Avalonia's

Book of Chakras

A practical manual for working with your chakras:
Using aromatherapy, colours, crystals, incense, mantra & meditation
to work with, balance and heal with your body's natural energy centres.

Published by Avalonia

BM Avalonia
London
WC1N 3XX
England, UK

www.avaloniabooks.co.uk

Avalonia's Book of Chakras
A Practical Manual for Working With, Balancing & Healing with Chakras
ISBN 1-905297-08-4

First Edition 2006
Copyright © Sorita D'Este & David Rankine

Design by Avalonia
Illustrations by Satori

"*From the self-combination of the Spirit which is Shiva and the Matter which is Shakti, and through their inherent interaction on each other, all creatures are born.*"

Siva Samhita 1.92

This little volume is dedicated to
The man who brought Chakras
And Tantra to the West

Sir John Woodroffe
(Arthur Avalon)

Table of Contents

Introduction

The chakras are energy centres in our subtle bodies, which have been used in Tantra in India for thousands of years. In the late nineteenth century westerners started discovering the beauty and complexity of Tantra, the oldest unbroken lineage of complex spiritual practice in the world. The detailed and rigorous system of the energy body found in the chakras, together with ways of working with them did not have a parallel in the Western Mystery Tradition, resulting in their incorporation into many modern systems such as Paganism, Wicca, Magick and the New Age movement.

Although the terminology used with the chakras may sound strange being in Sanskrit, the chakras are really a universal concept. Everybody has an energy body and there can be no discrimination on race, colour, social status or sexual preference when it comes to chakras. By focusing on the subtle energy of the chakras and your aura, you are indicating to the universe your determination to develop a holistic existence and through this explore the mysteries of spiritual growth and enlightenment.

When working with your chakras you obviously want as complete a picture of your energy body as possible, in the same way that you wouldn't go to a doctor and expect them to diagnose an ailment without giving them all the symptoms. For this reason we have included as much material about the minor chakras as we could, to enable you to build up a greater understanding of your own energy body and the way you can work with it.

For the same reason we have included extensive information on techniques for both stimulating and calming your major chakras. To enable you to have all your chakras in balance is the aim of this book. If you follow the exercises within, finding which work best for you, and develop a harmony in your energy body, your physical and emotional life will equilibrate to a similar harmony, and you will be able to take greater steps in pursuing your spiritual path.

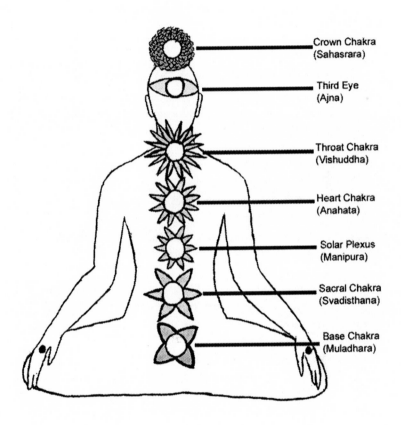

Crown Chakra
(Sahasrara)

Third Eye
(Ajna)

Throat Chakra
(Vishuddha)

Heart Chakra
(Anahata)

Solar Plexus
(Manipura)

Sacral Chakra
(Svadisthana)

Base Chakra
(Muladhara)

CHAPTER 1

What are the Chakras?

Much has been written and said about chakras, sometimes lucid and accurate and sometimes contradictory and confusing. To be able to effectively work with your chakras it is necessary to first have a good grasp of what the term means.

The chakras can be described as energy centres in our subtle bodies. The word chakra (or cakra) comes from the Sanskrit language and translates as "*wheel*" or "*disk*", a reference to the concept that our chakras each spin at a particular frequency when they are in harmony with our physical bodies.

At times the chakras are also described as being akin to lotuses, as they are said to have petals. The conscious opening of the chakras is considered to be a thing of great beauty, just like the opening of the sacred lotus flower. When the chakras are opened consciously, in harmony with each other, it signifies a person who is balance with both themselves, as well as with their spiritual path.

Today most people work with a standard system of seven chakras, six of these are found running up the spinal column from the base to the third eye, with a seventh at the top above the head (crown chakra).[1]

This seven chakra system dates from around fifteen hundred years ago and is commonly taught in the West today having been both adopted and adapted for use in many different spiritual practices. It is important to note at this point that that early Sanskrit texts give differing accounts on how many chakras there are in the human body and that many others are referred to in different parts of the body, in addition to those which run up the spinal column. These other chakras are known as the minor chakras, they are found all over the body, including at the feet, hands and sensory organs.

---

[1] "In this body, the Mount Meru [vertebral column] is surrounded by seven islands." Siva Samhita 2.1.

Each of our chakras are connected to each other through energy channels which are called Nadis. These run throughout the body and can be seen to function in a similar way to the veins in our bodies, governing the flow of energy throughout the subtle body. The term nadis can be translated as "*current*" or "*flowing water*" and there are said to be seventy-two thousand throughout the body, of which twelve are considered to be major nadis. All the nadis emanate from the Kanda, a bulb-shaped energy centre located just under the base chakra.

Of the nadis, the most prominent is the Sushumna, which rises from the base of the spine up to the third eye and contains the six major chakras from the base chakra through to the third eye chakra. Two other nadis also rise from the base chakra, these are:
- o The white lunar Ida
- o The red solar Pingala

The Ida & Pingala act as conduits for the feminine and masculine energies in the body. As they rise up through the body they create a criss-cross shape, crossing over the Sushumna and ending in the Ajna chakra. This shape made by the vertical Sushumna, with the Ida & Pingala intertwined around it, and the Ajna chakra, with its two petals, at the top, has been said to be the prototype for the well known western symbol of healing, the caduceus. The caduceus pictures two serpents intertwined over a central staff with a winged disk at the top and is associated with the Greek God of Healing, Asclepius.

Within the fiery red Sushumna there is a nadi called the Vajrini which is golden in colour, which contains within itself the white Chitrini nadi. The more spiritually developed a person is, the more luminous their Chitrini nadi is said to be. The Chitrini nadi is also sometimes called the "*royal road*" in reference to its function as the path the Kundalini ascends through.

Each of the seven major chakras also affects different parts of the physical body. This includes the glands that release the hormones in our bodies; the five senses, as well as specific parts of the physical body such as the skin, bones, muscles and blood.

The network of chakras and nadis generates the aura or subtle body that surrounds us. The aura is seen as being egg-shaped, slightly flattened around the middle, with a dent around the area of the solar plexus under the diaphragm (near the solar plexus or Manipura chakra). It is through this point that we absorb energy from the environment and interact with others through emotional energies.

Our chakras influence us across a wide range of levels, including the physical, emotional, mental, psychic and astral. This is why it is as important to care for our chakras as it is our physical bodies.

In addition to the chakras and nadis, our energy body also contains the Kundalini, or serpent power. The Kundalini is seen and described as a serpent coiled three and a half times at the base of the spine, in the base chakra. The word Kundalini is derived from the Sanskrit word kundali meaning "*spiral*". The three and a half coils are significant as it is also the number of times the serpents of the caduceus cross, and the spiral of the DNA double helix (the blueprint of human life) repeats every 3.5 A° (10^{-10}m).

The Kundalini represents one half of the divine polarity of every person, for she is perceived as being the spark of the Goddess within each of us. In the same way, the masculine divine is perceived as residing in the crown chakra of every person as the God Shiva.

The purpose of awakening Kundalini is to encourage her to rise up through each of the major chakras systematically, to ultimately unite with Shiva within us. The union of the masculine and feminine divine, God and Goddess produces a divine state of bliss. It thus comes as no surprise that Kundalini is also known as "*the glittering dancer*", showing the emphasis on her active movement, and also the play of light on her scales as she rises.

Stimulating the Kundalini to rise requires a lot of effort and dedication, sometimes months or even years of work. An entire branch of yoga, Kundalini Yoga, is dedicated to it and worth exploring if you wish to work towards this goal. Although not that common, Kundalini experiences can happen involuntarily. Such an experience can produce fear, together with profuse heat and sweating. The body may twitch and involuntary spasms may also occur, both before and after the ascent. Additionally the physical senses may become hypersensitive, resulting in discomfort from bright lights and loud noises.

The Kundalini will only rise up and pass through the chakras if they are in balance. As a result any of the chakras that are out of balance will halt the ascent of the Kundalini, resulting in only a partial ascent. As Kundalini enters a chakra, the deities of that chakra are said to merge with her, generating more energy and adding to the momentum of the ascent. This results in the ultimate union of all divine force within the body enabling us to connect to the divine outside of the body in bliss and union.

Each element of the body dissolves into the next higher element, as is described in the following extract from the Siva Samhita:

> "The earth (Muladhara) becomes subtle and dissolves into water (Svadisthana); water is resolved into fire (Manipura); fire similarly merges into air (Anahata); air is absorbed into ether (Vishuddha); and ether is resolved into avidya (removal of subject and object, Ajna), which merges into great Brahma (Sahasrara, ultimate bliss)."[2]

---

[2] *Siva Samhita 1.78.*

11

CHAPTER 2

Working with the Chakras

Each person we meet, each experience we have, and each thing we do, shape us into the people we are. In a similar way, our experiences affect our energy body and our chakras. Strong experiences, both positive and negative, may cause our chakras to become too open or too closed, leading to imbalances. These imbalances may in turn lead to health and emotional problems, and could also lead to personality disorders.

When we are born, our chakras tend to be naturally open, enabling us to receive constant input from the environment we live in. Experiences and events that take place around us eventually result in our chakras becoming partially, and in some instances, fully closed. This process usually starts with the upper chakras closing as a result of social conditioning which starts at an early age, when we are taught to view the world and behave in a socially accepted manner and to subdue our imaginations and control our emotions.

The lower chakras are usually less affected by social conditioning and may remain open, only closing when we find ourselves in a situation which is threatening to us or as a result of other negative experiences. The lower chakras may also close due a lack of stimulation, which often happens if we find ourselves in an environment which lacks encouragement towards reaching and setting goals, as well as achieving success through learning and new experiences.

Today, it is well known and accepted that childhood experiences can have a huge effect on our lives as adults. Children who experience bullying, constant criticism or neglect will experience feelings of inadequacy which will cause the lower chakras to close as a natural defence mechanism. Such experiences can also lead to feelings of alienation and depression which will lead to the upper chakras closing in children or adults who have not yet learned to cope with such traumas.

Through learning how to work with your chakras and how they function, you will be able to open and close them in the appropriate circumstances. This will enable you to you to keep a balanced state of mind and reduce your susceptibility to being influenced by people and situations over which you have no control and which may otherwise affect you in a negative way. It will also help you to improve your general health and enable you to work on long-term emotional and physical problems which often are the cause of distress over long periods of time.

Techniques for working with the chakras are generally simple, and easy to include in your life. The most common techniques, which will be given in more detail in the subsequent chapters, include using a combination of aromatherapy oils, colours, crystals, meditation and the voice. They do not require special training, but will require discipline and perseverance as you work through the different techniques in an effort to find the technique, or a combination of techniques, which work best for you.

Dietary Considerations

Food and stimulants can have a huge impact not only on our physical body, but also on our energy body. There are a few simple dietary considerations which are recommended for successful work with the chakras and these include:

o   Abstinence from stimulants (incl. caffeine, alcohol, sugar and tobacco)
o   Abstinence from meat
o   Fasting

Stimulants create an artificial peak in energy which cannot be sustained for long periods of time. This may result in imbalances and also makes it more difficult to sustain a balanced energy body. Abstinence from meat is also highly recommended, even if just for a few days prior to and during your chakra balancing work. Meat has a dulling effect on the body's psychic centres which is one of the reasons why a large percentage of people who practice Tantra and Kundalini Yoga are vegetarian.

13

Fasting is also a common practice in many spiritual traditions around the world and although longer periods will usually yield better results, we would recommend that food is avoided for at least four hours prior to energy work. Eating diverts energy into digestion and additionally makes it more difficult to balance the lower chakras, in particular the solar plexus. Please consult a medical doctor prior to undertaking prolonged periods of fasting.

Within the chapters on the major chakras is information on different ways of working with the individual chakras to balance their energies. The different methods within these categories are explored below:

Using Aromatherapy Oils

There are a number of different ways in which aromatherapy oils can be incorporated in chakra balancing work. Some methods work better for some of the chakras than others, for this reason the appropriate technique are listed in each of the major chakra chapters.

For all of the techniques using essential oils, they should be diluted in a suitable base oil, such as Sweet Almond oil, before applying it to the skin. Oils are usually diluted by adding 5-10 drops of essential oil to 20ml – 30ml of base oil. If you have sensitive skin increase the ratio of base oil to essential oil and remember to test for allergies first!

o   Massage
Unless you are a qualified masseuse, care should be taken when massaging others. For chakra work strokes should be applied in a gentle anti-clockwise manner to calm a chakra and in a firmer clockwise manner to stimulate or help unblock it.

o   Bath Oils
Dilluted oils can be added to bathwater for their balancing, stimulating or calming effects while you soak.

o   Oil Burners
A variety of oil burners are available today, typically these have a small bowl in which water with a few drops of essential oils are placed. The water and oil(s) evaporate when heated by the flame of a tealight. The oils are released over a period of time

and are diffused slowly making this an ideal method to combine with mantra or meditation.

o   Evaporator Spray
Oils are diluted in water and used in a pump-action bottle container to spread its effects quickly in a room.

o   Compress
These can be applied hot or cold to specific parts of the body, such as the back of the neck or brow for fast effect. This is a particulary good technique to use for the throat and third eye chakras.

o   Steam Inhalation
Oils are added to a bowl of hot water and breathed in. A towel can be held over the head and bowl whilst this is done to increase the efficiency. Make sure to take care to not burn yourself!

o   Pulse Points
Oils are diluted, usually in a higher essential oil to base oil ratio and applied to the pulse points around the body for area specific benefits.

Colours

For each chakra colours are given which help calm or stimulate that chakra, to use or avoid appropriately. These colours can be used in a variety of ways. You can wear the required colour so it is around you and thus affects your energy body. You can also use coloured bubble baths, or put a light bulb of that colour in rooms in your home to permeate the atmosphere, decorate rooms in appropriate colours or use furnishings to both help balance your chakras and for continued effect which is particular appropriate when correcting serious problems.

Crystals

Crystals act as extraordinary objects to focus energy and for this reason are often used in energy work and healing. For chakra work is it best to wear the appropriate crystal as near as possible to the appropriate chakra centre. However you will still receive the benefits of carrying the crystal on your person or wearing it as a piece of jewellery. It is however always preferable that the crystal is touching your skin if possible. Selections of crystals corresponding to each of the major chakras are given in their respective sections.

There are various ways of incorporating crystals into chakra work, in addition to carrying it on your person, for example, crystals can also be incorporated into meditations or used as a focus during mantra work. Of course, you may also want to work on more than one chakra at the same time, in such instances you should use a selection of crystals corresponding to the chakras you will be working with.

Following are some examples of methods which incorporate more than one crystal into chakra balancing work:

o   Energising Layout
    If a person is at low ebb and their chakras need a boost, use an energising layout which encourages the body to circulate energy around the whole aura. Place a carnelian at the pubic bone (base), a topaz at the solar plexus, a lapis lazuli at the throat and a zircon at the crown. Place four quartz points at the feet and hands, point inwards.

o   Star of Solomon
    Place six quartz points in a star, composed up interlocking upwards and downwards pointing triangles, around the chakra, with a suitable crystal which corresponds to the chakra you are working with, in the centre. Leave the crystals in place for 5-10 minutes. For example, if you wish to stimulate the base chakra you could place a carnelian in the centre over the chakra.

o   Whole Body Quartz Line
    For this place a crystal at each of the major chakra points on the body. Ideally you should lie face down, on your front, so the help of another person is required for this technique. The layout uses all crystals from the quartz family, which are sympathetic to each other and encourages the chakras to all balance and equilibrate.

Following a list of the chakras with a crystal which corresponds to it to use for this technique:

o   Crown - Quartz
o   Third Eye - Smoky Quartz
o   Throat - Amethyst
o   Heart - Rose Quartz
o   Solar Plexus - Citrine Quartz
o   Sacral - Tiger's Eye
o   Base - Carnelian

Crystal Gem Elixirs

Crystal gem elixirs are an excellent way to use the healing energy over a period of time for physical and emotional balance. If you wish to make an elixir to act on the body make the remedy in sunlight; and for emotional, mental and spiritual purposes moonlight is preferable. For further information on how to make your own gem elixirs please see Appendix 1 at the back of this book. Crystal gem elixirs are used in a similar way to flower remedies.

o   Drinking Gem Elixirs
The elixir should be diluted in a glass of water or fruit juice and drunk twice a day. Five drops of elixir to a glass of water is the usual dosage.

o   Tongue
Elixirs may also be applied directly under the tongue undiluted if you feel the need for a rapid effect

o   Other methods
You can apply the elixir directly to the body in the area you wish to target, or alternatively add a few drops to your bath water.

Gem elixirs may be used daily over a prolonged period of time and as it can be used easily in almost any circumstances, it is ideal to take with you on holiday.

Incense

Humans are very receptive to fragrance, and using incense, in the same way as with burning essential oils in an oilburner, you can surround yourself with the appropriate scent for the chakras you are working with. It can be incorporated into the home environment as well as in particular workings or ceremonies. Incense blends are made by blending resins, barks, oils and herbs together; usually this is done by grinding the ingredients together in a pestle and mortar. The resulting blend is then burned on a self-igniting charcoal block and the effects of the blend are released in the resulting incense smoke.

Mantras

The repetition of mantra is a very effective way to calm or stimulate your chakras and one which requires no external tools. Mantras are best done by intoning the words out loud, but can also be used silently in circumstances where it is not possible to chant out loud (such as the workplace!).

Meditation

Meditation is a great, yet simple tool which has long been used to help calm the mind, body and spirit, thereby creating a balanced state in which it becomes easier to focus. The meditations given in each of the major chakra sections can be used to focus the mind on individual chakras, making them useful when working on a specific chakra. With many added benefits, such as stress relief, meditation is a technique worth exploring in more depth if you are interested in doing advanced energy work.

Are Your Chakras Balanced?

How do you determine if your chakras are in harmony with each other? How do you know whether or not your chakras are out of balance and which ones need calming or stimulation?   Obviously these are important questions to ask right from the beginning: after all you will need to be able to determine if you have imbalances in order to be able to work towards healing and balancing them!

It is best to start by spending some time thinking about your own well-being:

- o   How do you feel emotionally?
- o   What is the condition of your own body and health?

Make a list of things related to both your physical and emotional state, being brutally honest with yourself. These will form a basis from which to work to determine which of your chakras are out of balance and may need attention.

Working through the major chakras one by one, go to the tables given in each section "Conditions of the ... Chakra" and read horizontally along the lines in the table of conditions and select the word in each line which is most appropriate for you. Then add up the number of appropriate words in each column, and see which has the greatest total. The column with the greater number of states relevant to you, at the time you do the assessment, is likely to be the state of that chakra.

It is very rare for a person to have all their chakras in harmony, so don't worry if you find more than one of your chakras seems to be out of balance. Remember that it is necessary for you to be brutally honest with yourself when examining yourself for this purpose otherwise the exercise becomes meaningless.

CHAPTER 3

Muladhara

The Giver of All Accomplishments
The Base Chakra

Overview of the Muladhara Chakra

The Muladhara or base chakra is located at the base of the spine, which is located at the perineum, between the anus and the genitals. Muladhara means *"root"* or *"support"* which is an appropriate descriptive term for the role of this chakra as the support upon which all the other major chakras rest and draw energy from.

The Muladhara chakra rules the adrenal glands. It is symbolically depicted as having four red petals which represents the four directions and the blood of life. The petals also represent the four states of: bliss in concentration, delight in controlling passion, great joy, and natural pleasure.

Inside these petals there is a circle containing the symbol for the seed-sound Lam in a golden yellow square, corresponding to the element of Earth. There is also an inverse red triangle, symbolic of the yoni of the Goddess, with its three sides corresponding to the Sun, Moon and Fire, and also the Sushumna, Chitrini and Vajrini nadis, which are indicated by an upward moving column with its inner divisions. The triangle sometimes also contains a lingam (sacred phallus) around which the Kundalini resides, coiled three and a half times. The nature of the polarity of the divine force within each of us is thus emphasised, being both male (lingam) and female (yoni and Kundalini).

In some of the portrayals, the base chakra is depicted as containing the seven-trunked sacred elephant Airavata. The seven trunks of this elephant correspond to the seven major chakras and to the power of Muladhara to activate the higher chakras when Kundalini is awakened. Airavata is depicted as being a brilliant white, which hints at the divine power that can be achieved from a position of strength

20

and perseverance, which are the qualities which are associated with an elephant.

The God Ganesha and the Goddess Dakini are both attributed to the base chakra. Ganesha, the elephant-headed God who removes all obstacles, is usually invoked in Hindu ceremonies before any spiritual practice. Shakti is the name given to the divine feminine energy, which manifests in all of the Goddesses, and at the base chakra she manifests as Dakini Shakti. Dakini represents the creative and protective urges, and she rules the skin, our largest organ of sensing. The divine feminine is also manifested in the base chakra as Kundalini, the fire serpent of creative energy who represents our drives and dynamism.

The base chakra is the centre of instinct, survival, pleasure and base sexuality. As the chakra of Earth, it has the attributes of this element, giving the quality of cohesive resistance and the weight of solidity. In the physical body the base chakra controls the sense of smell, the gonads and adrenal glands. The base chakra also governs the solid aspects of the body, such as the bones, teeth, nails and hair, and the excretory system, i.e. the disposal of waste products from the body.

At the level of being experienced through the base chakra, comes the experience of security and satisfaction in the current state and being comfortable with the status quo. As a result there is no urge to progress or create, which in turn may lead to inertia. This is why the Muladhara is also known as the *"plane of blind darkness"*, for it represents the unawakened soul, led by the desire for self-gratification of the senses. In the modern world we live in many people lead their lives with their base chakra open, but with all those above it closed.

The base chakra is strongly connected to our health and feelings of security. When the base chakra is blocked we can experience problems with our sex drive, and with lethargy, leading to susceptibility to illnesses like colds and flu's. When overactive it leads to selfishness and anti-social behaviour. Illnesses associated with imbalance in the base chakra include obesity, haemorrhoids, constipation, anorexia, degenerative arthritis, sciatica, knee problems and frequent illness.

Being bullied affects the base chakra, as it confuses the fight or flight state in the body. As a result the adrenal glands release adrenaline into the body which is not used, this may in turn contribute to blockages in the base chakra. Being neglected by family and friends, or being subjected to criticism may also cause this chakra to close down as self-esteem is damaged. To help open the base chakra and bring it into harmony with the rest of your body it is important to learn to value yourself and to be assertive, standing up for yourself when you need to.

Although the flow of energy upwards is often emphasised, it is important to remember that calling energy down from the crown chakra to the base chakra is as powerful as sending it upwards, as it helps us to ground our energies. By grounding we maintain our contact with the earth, with its boundaries, edges and limitations. Being grounded focuses us in the positive qualities of the base chakra and enables us to hold on to things and to contain, without this quality we become empty vessels.

The base chakra is linked directly to the minor chakras in the feet, which connects us to the earth beneath us, grounding us and keeping our perspectives realistic. This allows interaction with earth energies bringing to mind the expression: keeping your feet on the ground.

The base chakra is also linked to the coccygeal minor chakra, which is associated with physical vitality; and to the perineal minor chakra which links the sexual aspects of the base and sacral chakras.

Correspondences of the Muladhara Chakra

Animals	Bull, elephant, ox
Colour	Red
Element	Earth
Energy State	Solid
Foods	Proteins, meat
Force	Gravity
Goddesses	Dakini, Anat, Ceridwen, Demeter, Erda, Ereshkigal, Gaia, Lakshmi
Gods	Ganesha, Dumuzi, Geb, Hades, Pluto, Tammuz
Inner State	Stillness
Metal	Lead
Musical Note	C
Planets	Earth, Saturn
Seed Sound	Lam / Ra
Sense	Smell
Verb	I Have
Yoga	Hatha
Yoga Poses	All the balancing poses such as The Tree, The Dancer, The Eagle. Also seated meditation postures such as The Lotus and The Thunderbolt.

Conditions of the Muladhara States

Too Open (Excessive Energy)	Balanced Chakra	Blocked (Deficient Energy)
Bullying	Caring	Fearful
Materialistic	Focused	Difficulty achieving Goals
Reckless	Grounded	Over-cautious
Self-centred	Secure in Self	Needy
Over-confident	Self-confident	Insecure
Dissatisfied	Comfortable	Inert
Domineering	Strong	Vulnerable
Cynical	Happy	Fantasy-prone
Crude Behaviour	Balanced Behaviour	Obsessive compulsive

Aromatherapy

The essential oils for calming the base chakra are the antiseptic ones like cajeput, eucalyptus and tea tree. The stimulating oils are woody and fresh oils such as cedarwood, myrrh, patchouli, pine, peppermint, sandalwood and vetivert.

Oil Recipe: Calming the Base Chakra
>3 drops each of cajeput, eucalyptus and tea tree
>Blend with 10 ml base oil

Oil Recipe: Stimulating the Base Chakra
>6 drops pine
>3 drops peppermint
>1 drop myrrh oil
>Blend with 10ml base oil

Colours

Red is the primary stimulating colour for the base chakra, but other hot colours like orange and yellow will also help stimulate it. Conversely cool colours such as blue, light green and white will help calm the base chakra.

Crystals

Emerald, jade and rose quartz all act to calm the base chakra. Carnelian, garnet and ruby all act as stimulators for the base chakra.

Incense

Incense Recipe: Stimulating or Opening Base Chakra:
>10g Myrrh resin
>5 drops Cedarwood oil
>3 drops Patchouli oil
>3 drops Vetivert oil

Incense Recipe: Calming or Closing Base Chakra
>5g Benzoin resin
>5g Rosemary herb
>3 drops Eucalyptus oil
>3 drops Tea Tree oil

Mantras

Mantra to Calm the Base Chakra
To calm the base chakra chant the root mantra Lam, in its corresponding musical note of C if possible.

Mantra to Energise the Base Chakra
The mantras on the four petals of the base chakra are Varn, Sarn, Sharn, Sxarn which may be chanted as a sequence to help clear blockages and/or stimulate the chakra.

Meditation

Meditation to Stimulate the Base Chakra
Sit in a comfortable cross-legged position (or half lotus or lotus if you can manage it) and breathe deeply. Burn a scent that stimulates the base chakra, you can use either oil (patchouli, cedarwood or sandalwood) or incense (see recipes). Close your eyes and meditate for a few minutes. Feel your connection with the earth beneath you. As you breathe in draw up energy from the earth below through your feet chakras, and feel it flow up your legs to your base chakra, stimulating it gently.

Meditation to Calm the Base Chakra
To calm the base chakra, sit comfortably holding a piece of rose quartz to your base chakra, at the back of the spine at the base. As you sit, meditate and visualise yourself surrounded by a cool pink glow, like the colour of the rose quartz, and feel the calming energy of the rose quartz permeating your base chakra and balancing the energy. If you wish to stimulate the base chakra, use a piece of carnelian or garnet instead, and visualise yourself surrounded by a hot red glow like the fire of a ruby.

CHAPTER 4

Svadhisthana

The Remover of All Illness
The Sacral Chakra

Overview of the Svadhisthana Chakra

The Svadhisthana or sacral chakra is located in the spine just below the navel. The name Svadhisthana (or Swadhisthana) means "*sweetness*", and this chakra is associated with many of life's sweeter things like pleasure, sexuality, nurturing, creativity (including procreation) and change.

The sacral chakra is symbolically depicted with six scarlet petals, and the symbol for the seed-sound Vam with a white (lunar) crescent, corresponding to Water, in the central circle. The six petals symbolise six states or inclinations which need to be overcome on your journey - credulity, suspicion, disdain, delusion, false knowledge and pitilessness.

The animal of the sacral chakra is the Makara, a mythical creature which is a cross between a crocodile and a fish. It is depicted with its mouth wide open, showing how desire can swallow everything without discrimination.

The God Brahma, the God of creative energy, is attributed to this chakra. In humanity he is represented by the creative energies of the sacral chakra, and in particular the womb in women. Rakini Shakti is the aspect of the Goddess which rules the sacral chakra, embodying the drive to express ourselves through our emotions and creativity.

The sacral chakra is the centre of realisation of polarity, the balance of opposites, and also affects our desire to socialise and interact with others. The sacral chakra is associated with the element of Water, and influences flows in our bodies, like the circulatory system, and governs the bladder and kidneys.

At the sacral chakra the singleness of the base chakra becomes duality, our point becomes a line, and we develop a degree of freedom and complexity as we become aware of and realise our difference from others.

Polarity manifests itself at this chakra - male/female, night/day, etc. The polarity of opposites by its very nature creates movement, without movement there is inertia, entropy. Although in some ways manifest at all levels, socialization, sexuality, sensuality and the desire to reproduce form the kernel of this process, and so this chakra is particularly concerned with social interaction.

As this chakra is connected with pleasure, the level of being associated with this chakra is a very easy one to become stuck in. Hedonism satisfies our senses, but does not stimulate the urge to grow spiritually. For this reason the sacral chakra is the other common chakra with the base chakra that many people become stuck in.

Keeping the sacral chakra balanced enables us to appreciate the pleasures in life and be willing and able to accept change and create the life we want to live. It helps us to express ourselves openly, to be playful, sensual, nurturing or sexual as we desire. Through the sacral chakra can we taste the fruits of our actions.

The sacral chakra links to the ovary chakras in women. The ovaries control sexual development and the production of eggs, as well as controlling the levels of oestrogen and progesterone in the body. The creative impulse of life from the ovaries is mirrored in the creative and nurturing drives governed by the sacral chakra.

It is also linked to the pubic minor chakra which enables emotional expression of sexuality, and the perineal minor chakra which links the sexual aspects of the base and sacral chakras.Being made to feel guilty for things that weren't your fault by manipulative family and friends closes the sacral chakra. This includes traumas like sexual and emotional abuse. Such events damage the ability to trust others, and developing friendships that enable you to honestly express yourself help open this chakra. Blockages or under-activity of the sacral chakra can affect self-image and make you feel inadequate and oversensitive, damaging self-esteem.

Correspondences of the Svadhisthana Chakra

Animals	Fish, Makara, sea creatures
Colour	Orange
Element	Water
Energy State	Liquid
Foods	Liquids
Force	Magnetism
Goddesses	Rakini, Aphrodite, Mari, Tiamat, Venus
Gods	Brahma, Manannan, Neptune, Poseidon
Inner State	Tears
Metal	Tin
Musical Note	D
Planets	Moon
Seed Sound	Vam / Ma
Sense	Taste
Verb	I Feel
Yoga	Tantra
Yoga Poses	The Triangle, Forward Bends, The Shoulder Stand, The Plough and The Butterfly.

Conditions of Svadhisthana States

Too Open (Excessive Energy)	Balanced Chakra	Blocked (Deficient Energy)
Insensitive	Emotionally Balanced	Oversensitive
Manipulative	Trusting	Guit Complex
Sexual Predator	Passionate & Sensual	Impotent / Frigid
Sexually Aggressive	Sexually Open	Premature Ejaculation
Opinionated	Expressive	Self-critical
Fantasist	Creative	Inexpressive
Hedonist	Sociable	Isolationist
Domineering	Enjoys Pleasure	Pessimist
Zealous	Enthusiastic	Martyr
Controlling	Free-spirited	Negative

Aromatherapy

Citrus oils like lemon, lime, orange and petitgrain calm the sacral chakra. Floral oils like chamomile, jasmine, juniper and rose, and woody oils like benzoin, sandalwood and ylang ylang stimulate the sacral chakra.

Oil Recipe: Calming the Sacral Chakra
>   3 drops each of lemon and orange
>   4 drops of petitgrain
>   Blend in 10ml base oil.

Oil Recipe: Stimulating the Sacral Chakra
>   4 drops each of juniper and benzoin
>   2 drops of jasmine
>   Blend in 10ml base oil.

Colours

Orange is the colour to which the sacra chakra particularly responds for stimulation, though other hot colours like red and yellow will also stimulate it. Cool colours calm the sacral chakra, especially blue.

Crystals

Aquamarine, coral, moonstone and quartz all act to calm the sacral chakra. Blue stones like lapis lazuli, sapphire and sodalite stimulate the sacral chakra.

Incense

Incense Recipe: Stimulating or Opening Sacral Chakra:
>   10g Benzoin resin
>   2g Juniper berries (crushed)
>   6 drops Sandalwood oil
>   3 drops Ylang Ylang oil

Incense Recipe: Calming or Closing Sacral Chakra
>   10g Frankincense resin
>   2 drops Bergamot oil
>   5 drops Lemongrass oil

Mantras

Mantra to Calm the Sacral Chakra
To calm the chakra down vibrate the root mantra Vam, in the musical note of D if possible.

Mantra to Energise the Sacral Chakra
The mantras on the six petals of the sacral chakra are Bam, Bham, Mam, Yam, Lam, Ram, which are chanted as a sequence to energise the chakra to ensure it is at the correct vibration.

Meditation

Meditation to Stimulate the Sacral Chakra
Lie on the floor with your arms out at 45° to your body, and your knees bent so your feet are pulled up towards your body, with the soles touching each other.   This position will stimulate your sacral chakra. Now meditate for a few minutes on your sacral chakra and feel its energy moving like the tides flowing. Visualise orange energy flowing round your body from and back to your sacral chakra.

Meditation to Calm and Balance the Sacral Chakra
To clam your sacral chakra, start by anointing the pulse points on your wrists with frankincense oil. Sit cross-legged, breathe deeply and hold a piece of aquamarine or moonstone to your body just below the navel.

Close your eyes, relax and say *"Through balance I am open to change, and can create the future I desire."*   Repeat this a few times and allow the calming energy of the crystal to balance your sacral chakra.

Note: You can also use this meditation to stimulate the sacral chakra by using a blue stone such as lapis lazuli or sapphire.

CHAPTER 5

Manipura

The Protector of All
The Solar Plexus Chakra

Overview of the Manipura Chakra

The Manipura or solar plexus chakra is located in the spine midway between the solar plexus and the navel. It is sometimes incorrectly referred to as the stomach chakra, which is actually a minor chakra linked to it. Manipura means *"lustrous jewel"*, and this chakra is one of transformation, connected to our emotions and our willpower. The associated animal is the ram Mesha, showing the driving power of will associated with this chakra.

The solar plexus chakra is symbolically depicted with ten dark or black petals, likened to the colour of storm clouds, and the seed-sound Ram in an Inverse red triangle, corresponding to Fire. The ten petals represent ten more states to be overcome on the spiritual journey - shame, fickleness, jealousy, desire, laziness, sadness, dullness, ignorance, disgust, and fear.

The solar plexus chakra is associated with fire, the fire of digestion and the fire of the will. The solar plexus chakra is the centre of interaction with the universe, of the digestive process, and of the emotions.

When considered in conjunction, the solar plexus and sacral chakras are known as the *"plane that is a mixture of light and darkness"*. These two chakras being awakened indicates a desire to learn, yet still the spirit strives for coherence, and hence the mixture of light and darkness. This is why there is the attribution of sixteen states to these two chakras all of which need to be overcome and controlled on the spiritual journey.

The attributed God is Vishnu as the great preserver, who brings peace and does not tolerate egotism. In this role he maintains the balance of will and positive emotion in the solar plexus chakra. Lakini Shakti is the aspect of the Goddess ruling the solar plexus chakra, embodying the principles of fire and independence.

Manipura has the qualities of expansiveness and warmth, of joviality in ourselves. Whilst earth and water in the first two chakras are downward moving, we see upward motion now with the upward expansiveness of fire. This is the chakra of transformation, both through the combustive process of digestion and also through transforming the inertia of earth and water into action, energy and power.

In magick we must develop our will and power consciously, which we do through increasing our awareness and by disciplined magickal work. Powerlessness often arises through ignorance about how to change our behaviour appropriately to the situations we encounter. Working with this chakra produces feeling of power in ourselves which help our development.

The solar plexus chakra governs the digestive organs like the stomach, the liver, the gall bladder and pancreas. Lying behind the stomach, the pancreas secretes substances necessary for the digestion of food, and of note insulin which helps control the body's sugar levels. When this chakra is over-stimulated it can cause problems with excess blood sugar, the major cause of diabetes, and when under-stimulated it can affect digestion, resulting in stomach ulcers. It also governs the nervous system, its fiery energy corresponding to the electric impulses that fire down the nerves to make our bodies act.

By balancing the solar plexus chakra we work to achieve a balance between our emotions and intellect, and transform ourselves into the dynamic, successful, happy and creative people we want to be. The solar plexus is hence also connected with expansion, with widening our outlook to include others, and this also includes the sense of humour.

The solar plexus chakra links to several minor chakras. These are the diaphragmatic chakra associated with personal attitude to health, the navel chakra, which stores emotions, and the kidney chakras, which govern the kidneys.

Correspondences of the Manipura Chakra

Animals	Ram
Colour	Yellow
Element	Fire
Energy State	Plasma
Foods	Starchy foods
Force	Will
Goddesses	Lakini, Amaterasu, Athena, Bride, Minerva
Gods	Vishnu, Agni, Surya, Ares, Bel, Dionysus, Helios, Mars
Inner State	Laughter, joy, anger
Metal	Iron
Musical Note	E
Planets	Mars, Sun
Seed Sound	Ram / Da
Sense	Sight
Verb	I Will
Yoga	Karma
Yoga Poses	The Cobra, The Bow, The Cat, The Coil and The Twist.

Conditions of Manipura States

Too open (excessive energy)	Balanced Chakra	Blocked (deficient energy)
Over emotional	Centred	Easily distracted
Self-centred	Free	Dissociated
Irrational	Connected	Lethargic
Manipulative	Gentle Strength	Insecure
Sarcastic	Good Humoured	Lacking Humour
Controlling	Respectful	Subservient
Angry	Balanced	Needs Reassurance
Workaholic	Pragmatic	Lazy
Judgemental	Considered	Sycophantic
Superiority Complex	Self-confident	Inferiority Complex
Dissatisfied	Happy	Miserable

Aromatherapy

Floral oils like carnation, chamomile, lavender and rose calm the solar plexus chakra. Spicy oils like black pepper, cardamom, cinnamon, coriander and ginger should be used to stimulate this chakra.

Oil Recipe: Calming the Solar Plexus Chakra
> 4 drops each of chamomile and lavender
> 2 drops of rose
> Blend in 10ml base oil

Oil Recipe: Stimulating the Solar Plexus Chakra
> 3 drops each of ginger, black pepper and cinnamon
> Blend in 10ml base oil

Colour

Yellow is the stimulating colour to which the solar plexus particularly responds, though orange may also be used. Cooler colours like lavender and purple may be used to calm the solar plexus chakra.

Crystals

Amber, citrine quartz, opal and topaz are all good crystals to use to stimulate the solar plexus chakra. To calm it use colourless crystals such as quartz, zircon and diamond.

Incense

Incense Recipe: Stimulating or Opening Solar Plexus Chakra
> 10g Frankincense resin
> 2g Basil herb (dried)
> 1 crushed Cinnamon stick
> 4 drops Pine oil

Incense Recipe: Calming or Closing Solar Plexus Chakra
> 10g Myrrh resin
> 2g Lavender flowers (dried)
> 5 drops Geranium oil
> 2 drops Jasmine oil

Mantras

Mantra to Calm the Solar Plexus Chakra
To calm the chakra down chant the root mantra Ram in the musical note of E if possible.

Mantra to Energise the Solar Plexus Chakra
The mantras on the ten petals of the solar plexus chakra are Damm, Dhamm, Namm, Tam, Tham, Dam, Dham, Nam, Pam and Pham, chanted as a sequence. This mantra sequence helps ensure the chakra is boosted to the right energy level.

Meditation

Meditation to Balance the Solar Plexus
Stand comfortably and visualise a golden glow emanating from your solar plexus chakra, and spreading to fill your aura with golden light. Now slowly walk around the room, saying "I will be balanced" as you take each slow step. Maintain the image of the golden glow filling your aura as you do this. Continue for five minutes, and do this daily to stimulate and balance the solar plexus chakra.

Meditation to Calm the Solar Plexus
To calm the solar plexus chakra, sit cross-legged and hold a piece of quartz to your solar plexus. Breathe deeply, and as you exhale each time, feel the surplus energy from your solar plexus chakra going into the crystal. Do this for as long as necessary, and store the crystal in yellow silk, to be used on another day when you need to energise your solar plexus chakra.

CHAPTER 6

Anahata

The Accomplisher of All Purposes
The Heart Chakra

Overview of the Anahata Chakra

The Anahata or Heart chakra is located in the spine at the level of the heart. Anahata means *"unstruck"*,[3] and this chakra is our centre of balance. It is the centre of love, being and equilibrium, the source of harmony. The chakra is symbolically depicted with twelve red petals, and the seed-sound Yam in a gold-edged hexagram on a smoky circle, the focus of Air.

The twelve petals correspond to twelve states or inclinations, which include positive qualities as well as dangers which arise on the spiritual journey. These states are hope, care, endeavour, attachment, arrogance, languor, conceit, discrimination, covetousness, duplicity, indecision and regret. The black antelope sometimes depicted in this chakra represents the fleeting nature of mystical and spiritual experiences, which can flee with the speed of the antelope if they are not grasped with a firm balance

The God attributed to this chakra is Rudra, the unpredictable weather God who brings sudden change, his presence showing the changeability of our hearts and the need for maintaining balance in our centre of balance. Kakini Shakti is the aspect of the Goddess ruling the heart chakra, and she embodies spiritual creativity and purity.

The hexagram represents the balance of forces, the emotional forces of the lower three major chakras rising in the upward pointing triangle to unite with the intellectual and spiritual forces of the three upper major chakras which descend to meet them. The two groups of forces are balanced in the heart chakra.

---

[3] As in a bell being unstruck. The bell symbolises the heavens and spirit.

The golden colour of the hexagram also represents the energy of healing which is directed from the heart chakra to the hand chakras. The heart chakra is known as the "*plane of light*", for as the centre of balance its awakening indicates the spiritual balance of the seeker on their true path, the way illuminated by their beliefs and experiences.

The heart chakra is associated with the element of Air, and has the qualities of mobility, gentleness, lightness and harmony. These qualities are expressed through movement towards, as a relationship with or sympathy for. It is also associated with the sense of touch, and helps us to be in touch with ourselves and others in a balanced manner, i.e. to relate positively, which we often refer to as being "*in touch*" with someone, or with our own feelings. Conversely, too much energy put into relationship with others will produce oversympathy and anxiety.

In the body the heart chakra controls the thymus gland, and influences the heart, blood, vagus nerve, and circulatory system. The thymus is located just above the heart, and produces growth-stimulating hormones especially in early life when growth is so vital. It also stimulates the production of lymphocytes, contributing to the effective functioning of the body's immune system. As the centre of balance, the heart chakra being out of balance will affect the whole system, as will problems with the thymus gland.

The most significant link from the heart chakra is to the healing chakras in the hands. Nadis from this chakra run to chakras in the hands which may be used to direct energy as gold healing light projected from the Anahata. The heart chakra is also linked to a minor chakra between the shoulder blades, associated with ego and willpower, and the diaphragmatic chakra which is associated with personal attitudes to health

Being rejected and feeling unworthy of receiving love due to lack of affection and disinterested family cause the heart chakra to close. This damages the ability to nurture and can result in self-pity. Physical exercise and learning skills like healing that help others can encourage this chakra to open.

The heart chakra is the centre of balance in our bodies, between the lower chakras connected more with the body and the upper ones connected more with the mind. When the heart chakra is out of balance it leads to us *"losing touch"* with ourselves and our surroundings. An overactive heart chakra can lead to selfish, manic and impulsive behaviour.

When it is blocked or under-active it can result in lack of drive and motivation, and a tendency towards hypochondria. Illnesses associated with imbalances in this chakra are asthma, respiratory problems, high blood pressure, and heart conditions.

Correspondences of the Anahata Chakra

Animals	Antelope, dove, nightingale
Colour	Green
Element	Air
Energy State	Gas
Foods	Vegetables
Force	Love
Goddesses	Kakini, Aphrodite, Freya, Isis, Lakshmi, Maat
Gods	Rudra, Vishnu, Avalokita, Krishna, Aeolus, Asclepius, Shu
Inner State	Compassion
Metal	Copper
Musical Note	F
Planets	Venus
Seed Sound	Yam / Sa
Sense	Touch
Verb	I love
Yoga	Bhakti
Yoga Poses	The Locust, The Camel, The Cobra, The Fish and Pranayama.

Conditions of Anahata States

Too open (excessive energy)	Balanced Chakra	Blocked (deficient energy)
Impulsiveness	Liberty	Lack of drive
Self-loving	Loving	Feeling Unlovable
Vampiric	Healing	Hypochondriac
Manic	Happy	Melancholy
Possessive	Compassionate	Self-depreciating
Conditonal	Unconditional	Feels Unworthy
Punitive	Nurturing	Fears Rejection
Melodramatic	Balanced	Self-pitying
Inconsiderate	Considerate	Over-attentive
Controlling	Independent	Dependent

Aromatherapy

Herby oils are good to stimulate the heart chakra, such as clary sage, marjoram, rosemary and sweet thyme. Floral oils are good for calming the heart chakra, such as geranium, lavender, melissa, rose and ylang ylang.

Oil Recipe: Calming the Heart chakra
>   4 drops each of geranium and ylang ylang
>   2 drops of rose
>   Blend in 10ml base oil

Oil Recipe: Stimulating the Heart chakra
>   3 drops each of clary sage, marjoram and rosemary
>   Blend in 10ml base oil

Colour

Green is the stimulating colour to which the heart chakra is aligned. It also responds well to pink and gold (the healing colour). To calm it use red.

Crystals

To stimulate the heart chakra use crystals like aventurine, emerald, jade, rose quartz and watermelon tourmaline. To calm it use red stones like carnelian, garnet and ruby.

Incense

Incense Recipe: Stimulating or Opening Heart Chakra
>10g Frankincense resin
>½g Orange peel (dried and shredded)
>5 drops Mandarin oil

Incense Recipe: Calming or Closing Heart Chakra
>10g Benzoin resin
>3g Pine resin
>4 drops Marjoram oil
>4 drops Rosemary oil

Mantras

Mantra to Balance the Heart Chakra
To calm the chakra down chant the root mantra Yam, in the musical note of F if possible.

Mantra to Energise the Hearth Chakra
The mantras on the twelve petals of the heart chakra are Kam, Kham, Gam, Gham, Nnam, Cam, Cham, Jam, Jham, Nyam, Ttam. This mantra sequence helps ensure the chakra is balanced at the right energy level.

Meditation

Meditation to Stimulate the Heart Chakra

To stimulate your heart chakra, sit down and spend a few minutes chanting the mantra Yam or Sa. As you do so see your heart chakra as a bright green sphere about the size of a tennis ball at the level of your heart centred on your spine. See the sphere spinning clockwise like the world, with any discolourations or impurities shooting off it as it spins around.

Meditation to Calm the Heart Chakra

To calm your heart chakra, sit comfortably with your eyes closed. Be aware of your breathing, and with each in breath, see yourself breathing in pure white light. Feel it filling your body, cleansing and energizing you.

With each out breath, breathe out any tension or negativity you have in the form of a thick black smoke. Continue with the smoke gradually getting lighter, going through shades of dark grey to light grey, until there is no more smoke to come out, and you are breathing in and out pure white light.

41

CHAPTER 7

Vishuddha

The Provider of All Auspiciousness
The Throat Chakra

Overview of the Vishuddha Chakra

The Vishuddha or throat chakra is located in the spine at the throat. Vishuddha means *"purification"*, and it is the centre of dreaming and creativity through the voice. It is symbolically depicted with sixteen smoky petals, and the seed-sound Ham in the centre in a white circle, representing Aether (Spirit), contained within a double downward triangle representing the divine power of Shakti as the yoni.

As the centre of dreaming, it is the *"plane of the Moon"*, for dreams are the domains of the night, their flows governed by the tides of the Moon. Also this is hinted at by the animal sometimes shown in images of this chakra, a snow-white elephant, showing the control of the subtle faculties through applied patience and discipline.

Isvara, an aspect of Shiva as ruler of the universe, is the presiding God of the throat chakra, embodying the creative power of the lower chakras made manifest. Shakini Shakti is the aspect of the Goddess ruling the throat chakra, and bestowing the higher powers of memory, intuition and will.

The throat chakra is the centre of spirit, and is the place from where the four elements below are balanced and made active. Through balancing the four elemental chakras below, we can purify ourselves and take responsibility for our spiritual growth and interaction with others. It is the centre of active magickal power (through the voice). Vishuddha has the quality of space, and is the bridge between the thought processes of the Ajna chakra and the bodily processes of the lower chakras.

The throat chakra has the qualities of self-expression, communication and creativity. It is associated with the sense of hearing, the receiving of sound, which comes from the throat - making yourself heard. To fully express yourself, you need to hear what others are saying, not just to listen, but also to process, and the throat acts as a bridge between the conscious and unconscious mental processes of the upper chakras and the chakras below it.

In the body the throat chakra controls the Thyroid Gland, and influences the Lungs, Alimentary Canal, and the Hearing, Bronchial and Vocal Apparatus. On either side of the larynx is the thyroid, producing thyroxine, which controls the metabolic rate of the body – the effective conversion of food to energy.

Behind the thyroid gland is the parathyroid, which controls calcium levels in the bloodstream, essential for healthy bones, nails and teeth. As the centre of active power, the glands in the throat reflect this by their control of body form. Illnesses associated with imbalances in the throat chakra are thyroid problems, throat and ear conditions.

The throat chakra links to several minor chakras. These are the base of neck chakra, which acts as a bridge to the nadis in the limbs; the thymic chakra, which is associated with concentration and the immune system, and the Lalana (or Kala) chakra at the base of the mouth, which helps mediate the flow of downward spiritual energy

Blockages in the throat chakra can develop in childhood, if children are not allowed to express themselves and are ignored – children being "*seen and not heard*" syndrome. Being exposed to prejudice and being prevented from expressing your self will both negatively affect the throat chakra and cause it to close, as will regular experience of being let down. Learning to communicate clearly and discuss and debate issues will help stimulate the throat chakra to open.

The throat chakra is the centre of creativity and self-expression – enabling us to "*give voice*" to our opinions and ideas. When your throat chakra is blocked or under-active it can lead to problems

43

expressing yourself, leading to feelings of unhappiness, and also feeling cut off from the spiritual side of life as everything seems mundane.

Physically if the throat chakra is blocked or over-active we are more prone to problems connected with the throat, like laryngitis, coughs and colds. When the throat chakra is over-active it can lead to arrogance, self-righteousness and a tendency to ignore others.

Correspondences of the Vishuddha Chakra

Animals	Bull, elephant, lion
Colour	Bright blue
Element	Aether / Sound
Energy State	Vibration
Foods	Fruit
Force	Creativity
Goddesses	Shakini, Bride, Ganga, the Muses, Sarasvati, Seshat
Gods	Isvara, Hermes, Mercury, Thoth
Inner State	Connection
Metal	Mercury
Musical Note	G
Planets	Mercury, Neptune
Seed Sound	Ham / Se
Sense	Hearing
Verb	I speak
Yoga	Mantra
Yoga Poses	The Lion, The Shoulder Stand, The Plough, The Headstand, The Camel and The Fish.

Conditions of Vishuddha States

Too open (excessive energy)	Balanced Chakra	Blocked (deficient energy)
Overconfident	Self-confident	Inadequate
Ignore Others	Value Self	Lacking Self-esteem
Stubborn	Open	Denying
Ungrounded	Spiritually Aware	Ignores Spiritual
Controlling	Responsible	Often Embarassed
Self-righteous	Contented	Unhappy
Over-talkative	Good Communicator	Inexpressive
Arrogant	Mediator	Unreliable
Dogmatic	Creative	Inconsistent
Over-eager	Discerning	Dull

Aromatherapy

Antiseptic oils are good for calming the throat chakra, such as eucalyptus, peppermint, pine and tea tree. Woody oils are good for stimulating the throat chakra, such as benzoin, cajeput, frankincense, myrrh and sandalwood.

Oil Recipe: Calming the Throat Chakra
>   3 drops each of eucalyptus, pine and tea tree
>   Blend in 10ml base oil

Oil Recipe: Stimulating the Throat Chakra
>   3 drops each of frankincense and sandalwood
>   2 drops each of myrrh and benzoin
>   Blend in 10ml base oil

Colour

The throat chakra is stimulated by the colour blue, and calmed by dark orange and red.

Crystals

Amethyst, labradorite, lapis lazuli, sodalite, tourmaline and turquoise all stimulate the throat chakra. Aquamarine, moonstone and pearl may be used to calm it.

Incense

Incense Recipe: Stimulating or Opening Throat Chakra
>   10g Frankincense resin
>   1g Aniseed herb (dried)
>   2g Rosemary herb (dried)
>   3 drops Eucalyptus oil

Incense Recipe: Calming or Closing Throat Chakra
>   10g Myrrh resin
>   ½g Clove powder
>   ½g Nutmeg (crushed)
>   5 drops Lavender oil

Mantras

Mantra to calm the Throat Chakra
To calm the chakra down chant the root mantra Ham, in the musical note of G if possible.

Mantra to Energise the ThroatChakra
The mantras on the sixteen petals of the throat chakra are Am, Amm, Im, IIm, Um, Uum, Rm, Rrm, Lrim, Llrim, Em, Aim, Om, Aum, Aam, Ah. These may be chanted as a sequence to stimulate the chakra.

Daily Affirmation
If you feel unheard, try using mantra as a daily affirmation to restore that confidence by allowing yourself to speak and let the power within flow and be expressed. Say, *"I will speak up for myself, what I have to say is worth hearing, I will take responsibility for my needs and listen to the needs of others".*

Repeat this for five minutes, speaking clearly, and finishing on a loud exclamation, expressing your power.

Meditation

Meditation to Calm the Throat Chakra

To calm the throat chakra, meditate whilst holding an aquamarine or moonstone to your throat with both hands. This will encourage your body to direct more energy downwards from the throat chakra to the lower chakras via the heart chakra.

Meditation to Stimulate the Throat Chakra

Any voice work can help stimulate the throat chakra. An example of this is singing, such as chanting your first name (of if you have one, your magickal name). Using mantras, shouting, screaming, roaring and generally using the voice are all good to stimulate the throat chakra and help clear blockages.

CHAPTER 8

Ajna

The Enchanter of the Triple World
The Brow Chakra

Overview of the Ajna Chakra

The Ajna or brow or third eye chakra is located on the brow at the position of the third eye, i.e. about 1.5cm above the bridge of the nose, in the centre of the brow. Ajna means *"to know"* or *"to perceive"* which is appropriate as it is associated with the psychic senses and extra-sensory perception, such as intuition, telepathy, precognition, clairvoyance and clairaudience. The third eye chakra is often more active in women than men, which may be where the expression *"women's intuition"* comes from.

It is symbolically depicted with two lightning coloured petals, representing the union of the manifest and the unmanifest. Within the central circle, there is a downward pointing triangle representing the yoni. This is sometimes shown containing a lingam, again indicating the balance of female and male energies. Although not always depicted, above the triangle there is a quarter Moon representing consciousness and psychic power, surmounted by a golden bindu symbolising detachment from the purely physical world.

This chakra is the *"plane of nectar"*, indicating the purity and bliss of the spiritually active seeker, who has moved to a point of radiating the positive qualities of their path as well as walking it.

It is depicted with two petals, which correspond to the two sides of the brain, for which it is the bridge. The two petals together with the centre of this chakra correspond to the three Gunas (principles) of Sattva (purity), Rajas (activity) and Tamas (inertia), and which also correspond to Spirit, Mind and Body.

The third eye chakra is the centre of spiritual power in the body. The third eye is associated with the imagination, and is the chakra you use when you visualise the intent of a spell or when you are meditating on an image, and as such is the eye that can look inwards and outwards. The third eye chakra is not attributed to an element, rather it is associated with Light, hence the expression of *"seeing the light"* when you have a sudden flash of intuition or inspiration.

Paramashiva is the God ruling the third eye chakra, and he is an aspect of Shiva as the supreme self, the highest development of humanity before uniting with the divine in the crown chakra. Hakini Shakti is the aspect of the Goddess ruling the third eye chakra, she dispels fear and grants boons, bringing awareness of unity, for the final stage of the spiritual journey – the crown chakra.

In the physical body the third eye chakra controls the Pituitary Gland, and represents Intuition, governing the lower brain, the second (least dominant) eye, nose, and nervous system. The third eye is the last of the six major chakras located within the Sushumna. The pituitary gland is located at the base of the skull at the rear, and was previously called the *"master gland"*; it releases hormones influencing body chemistry, growth and metabolism. It also produces the hormone that stimulates lactation in mothers. The intuitive and spiritual energies of the third eye are reflected in the pituitary's influence on the whole body.

There are several minor chakras linked to the third eye chakra. TheChandra chakra is located between the third eye and crown chakras, and linked to spiritual states such as mercy, patience, gentleness and non-attachment. Also above the third eye chakra is the Manas chakra, which is linked to the senses (hearing, sight, smell, taste, touch) and sensations initiated through dreams and hallucinations. It also connects to the upper forehead chakra, about 2cm above the hairline, and governs the thalamus gland.

An absence of discipline, being discouraged from trying to achieve goals, inconsistent behaviour from family and being subjected to abusive behaviour all affect the brow chakra. Practices like yoga and meditation that develop self-discipline and inner harmony help open the brow chakra. Setting life goals and achieving them also helps greatly.

The third eye chakra is associated with the imagination and the psychic senses. Modern living can cause the brow chakra to become unbalanced very easily, as is seen by the number of people exhibiting the problems associated with a blocked brow chakra. When the third eye chakra is blocked or under-active it can lead to mental fatigue, depression, pessimism and cynicism.

When the third eye chakra is over-active it can lead deluded and fantasy prone behaviour. In the physical body an over-active brow chakra can cause headaches, including migraines, insomnia and nightmares. The third eye chakra is associated with mental and spiritual processes, so if it out of balance it can seriously affect your perceptions and behaviour.

Correspondences of the Ajna Chakra

Animals	Owl
Colour	Indigo
Element	Light
Energy State	Image
Foods	Mind-altering substances
Force	Imagination
Goddesses	Hakini, Athena, Hekate, Iris, Isis, Tara, Themis
Gods	Paramashiva, Apollo, Belenus, Krishna, Morpheus
Inner State	Intuiting
Metal	Silver
Musical Note	A
Planets	Jupiter
Seed Sound	Aum / So
Sense	Sixth
Verb	I See
Yoga	Yantra
Yoga Poses	The Shoulder Stand, The Headstand, The Corpse and Alternate Nostril Breathing.

Conditions of Ajna Chakra States

Too open (excessive energy)	Balanced Chakra	Blocked (deficient energy)
Ungrounded	Intuitive	Materialistic
Detached	Spiritual	Atheist
Fantasy-prone	Visonary	Unimaginative
Too selfless	Caring	Self-centred
Deluded	Imaginative	Unperceptive
Overly Optimistic	Realist	Pessimist
Effusive	Charismatic	Withdrawn
Foolish	Wise	Cynical
Illogical	Pragmatic	Logical
Manic	Calm	Depressed

Aromatherapy

Floral oils are good for calming the third eye chakra, such as chamomile, geranium, lavender, melissa, rose and violet. Herby oils like basil, clary sage, juniper and rosemary are good for stimulating the third eye chakra.

Oil Recipe: Calming the Third Eye chakra

>   3 drops each of chamomile and lavender
>   2 drops each of geranium and rose
>   Blend in 10ml base oil

Oil Recipe: Stimulating the Third Eye chakra

>   3 drops each of juniper and rosemary
>   2 drops each of basil and clary sage
>   Blend in 10ml base oil

Colour

Indigo and very deep blues are the colours the third eye chakra particularly responds to for stimulation. To calm it use amber or orange.

Crystals

Amethyst, lapis lazuli, quartz, rutile quartz and sapphire are all good crystals to use to stimulate your third eye chakra. To calm it use watery crystals such as aquamarine, moonstone or pearl.

Incense

Incense Recipe: Stimulating or Opening Third Eye Chakra
> 10g Benzoin resin
> 1g Rosemary herb (dried)
> 2 drops Eucalyptus oil
> 4 drops Geranium oil

Incense Recipe: Calming or Closing Third Eye Chakra
> 10g Acacia resin
> 2g Pine resin
> 3 drops Peppermint oil
> 5 drops Ylang Ylang oil

Mantra

Mantra to Calm the Third Eye Chakra
To calm the chakra down chant the root mantra Aum, in the musical note of A if possible.

Mantra to Energise the Third Eye Chakra
The mantras on the two petals of the third eye chakra are Ham and Ksham, which should be chanted as a sequence to stimulate the brow chakra.

Meditation

Meditation to Calm the Third Eye Chakra
Deep breathing, taking slow deep breaths, can help you regulate the oxygen flow in your body, which will help calm the third eye chakra down to its normal balanced rate. Breathe in to a count of eight, hold your breath to a count of four, and then breathe out to a count of eight. Do this for a few minutes and your mind and body will relax to a calmer state.

Meditation to Stimulate the Third Eye Chakra

To stimulate the third eye chakra, sit and meditate, holding a piece of amethyst to your third eye and move it in slow clockwise circles, gently rubbing the skin as you do so.

Feel the energy of the amethyst flowing into your brow, stimulating the third eye into activity. As you do this visualise purple energy flowing from the crystal to your third eye.

CHAPTER 9

Sahasrara

Perfect Bliss

The Crown Chakra

Overview of the Sahasrara Chakra

The Sahasrara or Crown chakra is located just above the top of the head. Sahasrara means *"thousandfold"*, referring to the thousand petals it is described as having. It is considered to have the God Shiva, Lord of Liberation who dances the dance of creation, sitting in repose in it. It is symbolically depicted with one thousand brilliant petals, in twenty rings of fifty petals.

This lotus is a miniature version of the lotus of creation, embodying the principle of *"As above, so below"*. This is seen in Indian art and literature, where we see the thousand-petalled gold lotus of creation:

> *"When the divine life substance is about to put forth the universe, the cosmic waters grow a thousand-petalled lotus of pure gold radiant as the sun. This is the door or gate, the opening or mouth, of the womb of the universe. It is the first product of the creative principle, gold in token of its incorruptible nature."*[4]

The God Shiva resides in the crown chakra, as the bringer of liberation and ecstasy. He destroys the old and outmoded to make way for new creation. Maha Shakti is the aspect of the Goddess ruling the crown chakra. She is the supreme Goddess, Kundalini Shakti in her highest form as she unites with Shiva to bring liberation and ecstasy.

The crown is the centre of evolution, the residence of the divine spark or Bindu, the focus of thought. The crown chakra is the link between the individual and divine wisdom and cosmic energy. It represents

---

[4] Myths and Symbols in Indian Art and Civilization, Zimmer, 1946, p90.

consciousness, and rules all the processes and actions of the body and mind. When the crown chakra opens it can bring feelings of bliss and union with everything in the universe, sometimes called nirvana or Samadhi. This is why the crown chakra is the *"transcendent plane"*, it is seen as containing the supreme light of liberation.

In most people the crown chakra never opens fully, and the other chakras need to be balanced for this to fully occur. In the physical body the crown chakra controls the Pineal gland, and governs the upper brain and the more dominant eye. Energy may be projected as white light from this chakra via the Ajna chakra.

The pineal gland lies deep within the centre of the brain, and produces melatonin, the hormone that regulates our internal *"body-clock"*. Melatonin affects the production of the hormones from the other glands. If this gland is out of sync, it can affect the whole body; in the same way that depression or isolation caused by crown chakra problems can result in the body suffering. This gland demonstrates the interconnectedness of our emotions and ideas to our physical state of health.

The crown chakra links to several minor chakras. The first of these is the Chandra chakra, which is between the third eye and crown chakras, and deals with spiritual states like mercy, patience, gentleness and non-attachment. Below the crown chakra is also the Manas chakra, which is linked to the senses, i.e. hearing, sight, smell, taste, touch, and sensations initiated from within through dream and hallucination.

In some texts another chakra is described as being connected to the crown, called the nirvana chakra, which is said to be the seat of the super-consciousness or genius potential within each person.

Not being given a healthy diet, resulting in lethargy, your decisions being ignored, and lack of expression of feelings and love in the family can close the crown chakra. Major traumas which have caused mental distress also affect this chakra, such as abuse or grief. To open the crown you need to put yourself first and enjoy your life. Illnesses associated with imbalances in the crown chakra are depression, alienation and confusion.

The crown chakra is the centre of consciousness, and represents our link with the divine. It also oversees all the processes in the body and mind, and so it is very important that the crown chakra be in balance.

A blocked or under-active crown chakra can lead to feelings of isolation, guilt and disempowerment, feeling in a rut and inadequate, leading to depression. An over-active crown chakra can result in egotism, obsessive and manic behaviours, which can lead to arrogant and domineering attitudes. The crown chakra is our link to the divine in the universe, so when it is out of balance the effects on us can be severe.

Correspondences of the Sahasrara Chakra

Animals	None
Colour	Violet
Element	Thought
Energy State	Information
Foods	Absence of food – Fasting
Force	Enlightenment
Goddesses	Maha Shakti, Ennoia (Gnostic personification of Thought), Inanna, Nuit
Gods	Shiva, Odin, Zeus
Inner State	Bliss
Metal	Gold
Musical Note	B
Planets	Uranus
Seed Sound	Hung / Gn
Sense	N/A
Verb	I know
Yoga	Jnana, Meditation
Yoga Poses	The Headstand, The Lotus, all Meditation Poses.

Conditions of Sahasrara Chakra States

Too open (excessive energy)	Balanced Chakra	Blocked (deficient energy)
Manic Depression	Equilibrium	Depressive
Frustration	Empowered	Disempowered
Arrogant	Gracious	Indecisive
Over-friendly	Compassionate	Alienated
Manic	Efficent	Fatigued
Nymphomania	Sexually Happy	Sexually Confused
Needy	Happy	Isolated
Always Dissatisfied	Fulfilled	Unfulfilled
Obsessive	Focused	In a Rut
Egotistical	Spiritually Aware	Materialistic
Over-confident	Self-assured	Inadequate
"God" Complex	Connected	Loss of Identity

Aromatherapy

Floral oils, such as jasmine, lavender, lotus and rose, calm the crown chakra. Citrus oils are good to stimulate the crown chakra with; these include bergamot, grapefruit, lemon, lime and neroli.

Oil Recipe: Calming the Crown chakra
>   3 drops each of lavender and lotus
>   2 drops each of jasmine and rose
>   Blend in 10ml base oil

Oil Recipe: Stimulating the Crown chakra
>   4 drops neroli
>   3 drops each of lemon and lime
>   Blend in 10ml base oil

Colour

The crown chakra is stimulated by the colours violet and purple. Pale yellow is particularly good to calm it. When the crown chakra is imbalanced, it often affects the lower chakras, making them spin more slowly, resulting in lethargy and inertia. By concentrating on wearing and surrounding yourself with the warm colours like red, orange and yellow that stimulate the lower three chakras, you encourage them to rebalance.

With the other chakras balanced, it encourages the crown chakra to find its natural balance again. When doing balancing work to help harmonise the crown chakra, you should avoid cold colours, such as blue, during this time. Black should also be avoided.

Crystals

Diamond and zircon are particularly good for stimulating the crown chakra, as is tourmalinated quartz (quartz with inclusions of tourmaline). To calm it use crystals like citrine quartz or topaz.

Incense

Incense Recipe: Stimulating or Opening Crown Chakra
>10g Frankincense resin
>2g Lavender petals
>5 drops Lotus oil
>5 drops Rosewood oil

Incense Recipe: Calming or Closing Crown Chakra
>10g Benzoin resin
>1g Basil herb (dried)
>2 drops Bergamot oil
>3 drops Black pepper oil

Mantras

Mantra to Calm the Crown Chakra
To calm the crown chakra down, chant the root mantra Om (Aum), in the musical note of B if possible, or use the mantra Om Mane Padme Hum (*"The jewel in the lotus"*). The thousand petals of the crown chakra do not have mantras on them.

Mantra to Energise the Crown Chakra

To energise and balance the crown chakra, chant the mantras for each of the previous six chakras from the base to the third eye in turn, followed by Om at the end.

Meditation

Meditation to Calm the Crown Chakra

Meditation can calm an overactive crown chakra. Meditate holding a crystal that encourages balance, like jade, malachite, rhodonite or rose quartz. Allow the calming feeling of the crystal to spread through your body, and feel yourself floating, as if you are in a great white cloud. As you drift allow your crown to calm down.

Note: If you find yourself feeling too "*floaty*", think of the crystal and allow its presence to bring you back to your normal thoughts.

CHAPTER 10

What are the Minor Chakras?

In addition to the better known seven major chakras, there are also many minor chakras throughout the body. The best known of these are listed below with their functions. The minor chakras in the upper body are connected with our perceptions, emotions and intellect, such as those in the ears, eyes, shoulder, elbows and breast, and also our physical health, such as the clavicle, thymus and breast chakras.

The hand chakras are a special case, as they are the points of focus for our energies when we direct them, and are located in our prime means of manipulation our environment through touch and action. This is why the hand chakras link via the arm nadis (energy channels) directly to the point of balance at the centre, i.e. the heart chakra.

The minor chakras in the lower body are important for the functioning of the body as an organism. The minor chakras in the trunk of the body are linked in with the lower major chakras, and most of them are connected with the efficient functioning of major organs, like the liver, spleen, pancreas and kidneys.

Through these they help the body process toxins and waste materials, and ensure it runs smoothly, helping encourage the immune system when it needs it. Some minor chakras are involved with our fertility, such as the ovary and gonad chakras. Other minor chakras deal with our emotional well-being, particularly the lower limb chakras like the thigh, knee and feet chakras.

Nirvana

The Nirvana chakra has one hundred white petals and resides between the Sahasrara and Chandra chakras. It is connected to the pineal gland, and said to be the place where the soul leaves the body at death.

Chandra

The Chandra chakra has sixteen white petals and is also known as the *"Soma"* chakra or *"Indu"* chakra, and as the *"Fulfiller of All Expectations"*. It is located between the third eye and crown chakras, and deals with spiritual states like mercy, patience, gentleness and non-attachment.   This is reflected in the states associated with the sixteen petals, which are mercy, gentleness, patience, dispassion, constancy, prosperity, cheerfulness, rapture, humility, meditation, restfulness, gravity, enterprise, emotionlessness, magnanimity and concentration.

Manas

Directly above the third eye and below the Chandra chakra is the Manas chakra, which has six petals, which are linked to the senses, i.e. hearing, sight, smell, taste, touch, and sensations initiated from within through dream and hallucination.   The petals are said to be white during waking and black during sleep. It also governs the Thalamus gland.

Lalana

At the roof of the mouth is the Lalana chakra, with twelve red petals, which helps mediate the flow of spiritual energy through the body. The petals of Lalana represent the states of faith, contentment, sense of error, self-command, anger, affection, sorrow, dejection, purity, detachment, agitation or action, and appetite or desire. This chakra is activated by the mantra Aum. The Lalana chakra is also known as the *"Kala"* chakra or the *"Talu"* chakra, and as *"The Agitator of All"*.

Ears

The ear chakras are associated with balance in its different forms, being the subtle equivalent of the inner-ear. They help keep the two sides of the body in balance, help us to maintain our emotional equilibrium (*"keeping a balanced perspective"*), and on a physical level with not falling over!

The ear chakras are a maroon color, with an unspecified number of petals. We visualise four petals, as this is most often the number associated with minor chakras which are not clearly stated as having a specific number of petals.

Eyes

Just behind each eye are the eye chakras, which are linked to the third eye chakra on the brow, making a triangle of perception. As the third eye deals with our sixth sense and intuition, the eye chakras receive all the cues we take in from our environment, both consciously and unconsciously.

Clavicle

Located in the dip at the base of the neck where the clavicles meet, the clavicle chakra is associated with respiration through the windpipe and bronchial tubes. This chakra is also linked with the lungs, and is stimulated to help treat respiratory conditions like bronchitis and asthma.

Breasts

The breast chakras are located at the upper breast on each side, and deal with responsibility and nutrition. Unsurprisingly these chakras are most active in nursing mothers. Being so close to the heart chakra, they are also associated with balance, through the need to be responsible for your actions and body (nutrition).

Thymus

The thymus chakra is directly linked to the heart chakra, and has three white petals. Although the heart chakra is the centre of balance and is hence is linked to the immune system, this minor chakra deals exclusively with the immune system as well. This chakra is stimulated in healing techniques like Reiki to encourage the body's immune system into action.

Hrit

The Hrit chakra is located under the heart chakra, and has eight golden-red petals. It contains the Wish-fulfilling Tree, which is the vessel for realisation of the wishes of the seeker.

Shoulders

The shoulder chakras are located just above the chest, below the clavicle on each shoulder. They correspond to our connection with the world, being also linked to the crown chakra. So the side of the body which is dominant (i.e. right for right-handed, etc) will usually be the more active connection, and the other side the more passive connection.

Elbows

The elbow is one of the hardest and yet most vulnerable parts of the body. So it is not surprising that the elbow chakras should be connected with healthy relationships, which require us to be considerate of others whilst maintaining our own boundaries and identity in a positive manner.

Hands

The hand chakras are located in the palm of each hand. They link directly to the heart chakra, and are also known as the healing chakras, due to their use to direct healing energy. Especially important for people practicing healing techniques that direct energy or use the hands like massage and Reiki.

Some modern sources suggest the hand chakras being gold and silver, i.e. solar and lunar, however if this is the case the colours would be different. Looking at the energy in the appropriate nadis, the Ida and Pingala, then the dominant (solar) hand would have a red chakra, with the non-dominant (lunar) hand having a white chakra.

Diaphragmatic

The diaphragmatic chakra helps stimulate the pancreas, and encourages the circulation of the blood around the body. It also acts as a bridge between the heart chakra and the lower three major chakras, helping encourage our awareness of our bodies and our physical place in the universe. It has twenty-four yellow petals.

Navel

The navel chakra, at the navel, helps store emotions, hence the old expression *"gut feeling"*. It has six orange petals.

Stomach

The minor stomach chakra helps deal with digestion, particularly the digestion process in the large intestine as the food is processed. Stimulating this chakra helps encourage digestion and may ease digestive problems.

Liver

The liver chakra is linked to the proper functioning of the liver, helping to encourage the disposal of toxins from the body, and the production of the chemical substances which ensure the healthy functioning of the body by regulating the glands in the endocrine system.

Spleen

The two spleen chakras are linked to the workings of this organ, helping to regulate the balance of toxins in the body, and helps encourage their disposal. On a subtle level stimulating these chakras can encourage you to see what is bad for you, and any destructive patterns you tend to repeat.

Kidneys

There are two kidney chakras, located at these organs, which help govern the working of the kidneys. They each have ten red petals.

Ovaries/Gonads

The ovaries and gonads chakras are directly linked to fertility through encouraging those parts of the body in the production of eggs and sperm in the physical body. They are also associated with sexuality, being linked to the sacral chakra in women (the ovary chakras) and the base chakra in men (the gonad chakras). This may be why men associate sex with pleasure and women associate sex with love.

Perineal

Between the base and sacral chakras is the perineal minor chakra which links the sexual aspects of these two major chakras. It has four red petals.

Pubic Minor

At the front of the body at the pubic bone is the pubic minor chakra which enables emotional expression of sexuality. It has four red petals.

Coccygeal

Near the base chakra at the coccyx is the coccygeal minor chakra, which is associated with physical vitality. It has four golden yellow petals and is associated with the element of Earth.

Thighs

Halfway up the thighs are the thigh chakras. These chakras deal with self-confidence and personal strength. A lack of self-confidence is often tied in with feelings of insecurity about appearance, mobility and capability to achieve goals. Stimulating the thigh chakras helps to overcome feelings of inadequacy and the resulting problems.

Knees

The knees are one of the most crucial yet vulnerable parts of the body, essential for movement. The knee chakras are linked in to your flexibility, in the way you approach life and deal with situations.

Stimulating the knee chakras can help deal with issues like fear of change, egotism and fear of death.

Feet

Your feet connect you to the earth, and the feet chakras are connected to the base chakra. Through this connection the feet are linked to the rest of the body, which is how reflexology works, and the feet chakras need to be kept in balance to enable you to *"keep your feet on the ground"*. See the feet chakras with four deep crimson red petals each.

CHAPTER 11

Working with the Minor Chakras

The following techniques can be incorporated in your chakra work, healing work or other ceremonies to enhance the energy flow from a particular minor chakra point. Although many of them seem to be simplistic, it is good to experiment and work with them over a period of time.

Using the Hand Chakras

Rubbing your hands together and generating energetic heat between them, is a simple and effective way to open the hand chakras. This will help you prepare for directing energy through them.

Hands on Thighs

Rest your hands palm down on your thighs to direct the flow of energy towards stimulating your thigh chakras. Streghtening the thigh chakras in this way can help you to also strengthen your self-confidence.

Hands on Knees

Rest your palms of your hands on your knees to stimulate the knee chakras. This will help reduce the effects of resistance to change and ego inflation by making you more receptive to the transformation that ceremony can bring.

Hands on Feet

Sit cross-legged and hold your feet with your hands, so that your fingers curl comfortably over your toes and the palms of your hands rest against the soles of your feet. This position creates a closed energy circuit, enabling you to focus your mind and will help you to concentrate or visualise better.

Hands on Navel

If you are having a particularly intense positive experience, such as a powerful insight or realisation, or sense of the divine, place your palms over your navel, to store the positive emotional energy in your navel chakra. This will also help to strengthen your emotional self.

Using the Lalana Chakra

To help increase your energy during energies, touch the tip of your tongue to the roof of your mouth when you are not using your voice. This will stimulate the Lalana chakra, encouraging the flow of spiritual energy throughout the whole of your your body.

Using the Diaphragmatic Chakra

If you are struggling to feel centred after a powerful experience, such as a meditation because your energy is still affecting your mental process or emotions, causing you to feel disassociated, you can ground yourself by using the diaphragmatic chakra. This can be done by visualising the twenty-four yellow petalled chakra at your diaphragm. Do this whilst holding your palms to your diaphragm which will help the energy flow back to your bodily awareness.

CHAPTER 12

Further Work with the Chakras

There are many ways of working with and balancing your chakras, the following example can be adapted for personal use. We would recommend that if you are new to working with chakras you first familiarise yourself with these exercises before adapting them, this will ensure that you gain a good practical understanding of the energies you are working with first.

Pentagram Chakra Balancing Exercise

This exercise is a simple but potent one which keeps the energy body balanced and whole through regular practice, and can also be used for energising and ensuring clear boundaries before other work. The pentagram symbolises man, with his five limbs and five senses in balance with each other. Make sure that you are sitting comfortably with your back straight before starting:-

Visualise the base chakra as a disk of spinning red light, and when you see it clearly, inscribe an upright pentagram of gold light on the disk, vibrating (either silently or aloud) the seed sound for the chakra, RA. Then move to the second chakra and visualise it as a disk of spinning orange light, and when it is clear, inscribe an upright gold pentagram on it, vibrating the seed sound, MA.

Continue up the spine, to the solar plexus chakra, visualising it as a spinning disk of yellow light, and when you see it clearly inscribe an upright gold pentagram on it, vibrating the seed sound, DA. Next move up to the heart chakra, visualising it as a spinning disk of green light, and when it is clear inscribe an upright gold pentagram in it as you vibrate the seed sound SA.

Keep moving up the spine, to the throat chakra, which you should visualise as a spinning disk of bright blue light, and when seen clearly, inscribe an upright gold pentagram on it as you vibrate the seed sound, SE (pronounced SAY). Next move to the brow, and visualise the third eye chakra as a spinning disk of deep indigo light, and when you see it clearly inscribe an upright gold pentagram on it, vibrating the seed sound SO.

Finally visualise the crown chakra as a spinning violet disk above your head, with the bottom of the disk just brushing the top of your head. When you see it clearly, inscribe an upright gold pentagram on it and vibrate the seed sound HUNG. After having inscribed the pentagram on the crown chakra, imagine each pentagram was a seed, and visualise that seed bursting forth gold light, surrounding the body and filling the aura. When you can feel the gold light surrounding your body, concentrate the energy on any areas of the body which are in pain or feel weaker.

We recommend this exercise be done every day, irrespective of any other magickal work which you may be doing. If it is built in to the daily routine, it will greatly strengthen your energy body. If you find yourself in an environment which is unpleasant or distasteful to you in some manner, try adding an extra part onto the end of the exercise, where you visualise the outside of your energy body to be like a mirror, reflecting anything negative back to its source.

Chakra Healing Energising Exercise

If you plan to perform healing work, you can use the previous exercise, continuing when you have finished it with the following exercise. It draws together the energies of the Earth and Stars as Gold and Silver light at your heart chakra:

Focus your mind on the chakras in your feet. Vibrate the mantra HUM and feel the feet chakras drawing up energy as gold light (to symbolise the liquid molten core of the earth) from the earth beneath you with each in-breath. Visualise the feet chakras as deep crimson disks spinning on your feet horizontally flat rather than vertically. Now see the energy rising up through your legs and the base, sacral and solar plexus chakras up to the heart chakra.

Subsequently, concentrate on your crown chakra drawing energy into it, from the heavens above you as silver light with each out-breath. Bring the energy down through the third eye and throat chakras to the heart chakra.

See the gold and silver energies swirling together and blending at your heart chakra, and continue to draw up earth energy as gold light on the in-breath, and draw down stellar energy as silver light on the out-breath. Continue doing this until you feel full of healing vitality which you can then use for healing work you have planned.

With practice you should find that it becomes easy to continue this visualisation whilst healing, this is particularly valuable in a situation where you need a lot of energy, and also ensures you do not make the mistake of draining yourself through using your own energy.

Chakra Opening Exercise

For this exercise, as before, you should be sitting comfortably with your back straight. During the exercise you visualise your chakras as looking like flower buds which are slightly open. As the chakras are never fully closed, unless you feel the need to be completely detached from your environment, their usual state is a degree of openness. The degree of openness will depend on your way of dealing with the world.

Visualise your feet chakras as deep crimson flower buds, like a partially closed rose, one in each foot. See them both opening their four petals, and as they do so, vibrate the mantra HUM four times. (Note the feet chakras may be more open than the others, as they are your connection to the earth and usually remain quite open) Feel the energy rising up your legs, as twin golden pillars that rise up your legs and curve in to the base chakra at the base of the spine. When you feel the energy has reached the base chakra, see it as a slightly open red flower bud, opening its four petals as you vibrate the mantra RA four times.

Feel the golden energy start to rise up your spine, to your sacral chakra, which you see as an orange flower. See it open its six orange petals as you vibrate the mantra MA six times. Be aware of the golden energy continuing to ascend your spine, to your solar plexus chakra. See the ten yellow petals of the solar plexus chakra open as you vibrate the mantra DA ten times.

See the golden energy continue its ascent up your spine to your heart chakra. See the twelve green petals of the heart chakra open as you vibrate the mantra SA twelve times. From here feel the golden energy rise to your throat chakra, and see it open its sixteen blue petals as you vibrate the mantra SE sixteen times.

From the throat, see the golden energy rise up to your brow, to your third eye chakra. See the two indigo petals of the third eye chakra open as you vibrate the mantra SO twice. Then see the golden energy rise up to the crown of your head, and see the thousand violet petals of the crown chakra open as you vibrate the mantra HUNG fifty times.

Although there are a thousand petals, it would take a very long time to recite the mantra a thousand times, and it os often represented with fifty petals. Fifty is also a number of completion in the same way as one thousand, representing the fifty letters of the Sanskrit alphabet, and the fifty petals of the six major chakras from the base to the third eye.

Chakra Closing & Balancing Exercise

To close the chakras, you simply perform the reverse of the previous opening exercise. Note that when you see the chakra petals closing, they do not close completely but to a slightly open state, so you can still interact with the energies of your environment and other people.

See your crown chakra as an open thousand-petalled violet flower, and vibrate the mantra HUNG fifty times as you see the petals closing to a slightly open bud state. Move down to your third eye chakra, seeing it as an open two-petalled indigo flower, and see the petals closing to the slightly open bud state as you vibrate the mantra SO twice. Keep moving down to your throat chakra, seeing it as an open sixteen-petalled blue flower. Visualise the petals closing to the slightly open state as you vibrate the mantra SE sixteen times.

Now move your attention down your spine to the heart chakra, seeing it as an open twelve-petalled green flower. Visualise the petals closing to the slightly open bud state as you vibrate the mantra SA twelve times. Continue down to your solar plexus chakra, seeing it as an open ten-petalled yellow flower. Visualise the petals closing to the slightly open bud state as you vibrate the mantra DA ten times.

Continuing down, see the sacral chakra as an open six-petalled orange flower. Visualise the petals closing to the slightly open bud state as you vibrate the mantra MA six times. Continue to move down to the base chakra, seeing it as an open four-petalled red flower. Visualise the petals closing to the slightly open bud state as you vibrate the mantra RA four times. Finish by moving down to the feet chakras, seeing them as open deep crimson four-petalled flowers. Visualise the petals closing to a half-open state as you vibrate the mantra HUM, remembering these chakras are usually more open than the others.

Elemental Chakra Meditation

This exercise uses elemental symbols from within the chakras. It can be very distracting to try and time things exactly whilst concentrating on visualisations and directing your breath, so you might like to try using a mala. A mala is a string of beads used for reciting mantras, usually with 108 beads on. If you time beforehand how long it takes to move the beads through your hand for one complete circuit from the counter bead back, you can use multiples of complete counts to time yourself. This is easier as you do not have to count as you do it, the counter bead acting as the prompt that you have completed a cycle, as it is the start and end point.

Sit comfortably on the floor, preferably cross-legged so your bum is in contact with the floor. Visualise the yellow square of Earth at your base chakra, and for two minutes breathe with a regular rhythm, focusing on sending the breath all the way down to the base of your spine. During this time concentrate on the element of Earth and its qualities.

Next visualise the white crescent (horns up) of Water at your sacral chakra, and for four minutes breathe with a regular rhythm, focusing on

73

sending the breath down to the sacral area. Concentrate on the element of Water and its qualities during this time.

Move on to the red equilateral triangle (point down) of Fire at your solar plexus chakra, and for six minutes breathe with a regular rhythm, focusing on sending the breath down to the solar plexus. Concentrate on the element of Fire and its qualities during this time.

Continue with a gold hexagram of Air at your heart chakra, and for eight minutes breathe with a regular rhythm, focusing on sending the breath to the heart. Concentrate on the element of Air and its qualities during this time.

Finally visualise a white circle of Spirit at your throat chakra, and for as long as is comfortable breathe with a regular rhythm, focusing on the breath in the throat. Concentrate on the element of Spirit and its qualities during this time.

The Wish-fulfilling Tree Exercise

This exercise is a creative visualisation to achieve goals that you which to achieve. Be realistic in your wishes, and they are more likely to succeed (e.g. a new job is much more realistic than winning the lottery). Remember that when you send energy to realise a wish, you also need to give that wish avenues to manifest in your life, and be open to the opportunities that may arise.

It is a good idea to prepare a mental image of the wish you want to realise beforehand, so when you reach that part of the meditation you have a sharp and defined image to focus the energy on. Clarity and precision make all the difference when performing creative visualisations.

Sit comfortably, and visualise your Hrit chakra. It has eight golden-red petals, with a tree in the centre, and is located between your Heart chakra and your Solar Plexus chakra. Focus your awareness on the wish-fulfilling tree in the centre of the chakra. When you are clearly focused on the tree, see it growing larger and merging with your body, so you become the tree. Feel your body as your trunk, your arms as your branches. Then start to put forth roots from your feet, down into the earth. Deeper and deeper into the earth, through the layers of rock, through the underground streams of water, through pockets of air within the earth, ever deeper until you reach the molten core, the fire at the centre of the earth.

From the core, with every in-breath you take, draw forth sparks of golden energy, up into your roots, drawing the energy up into your trunk. Do this for a couple of minutes, drawing up more and more of the golden earth energy. Then feel the energy of the heavens, of the sun and moon and stars, on your leaves. With every out-breath draw down silver sparks of heavenly energy, drawing it down through your branches, into your trunk.

Continue drawing in energy, so that with every in-breath you draw up gold sparks from the earth, and with every out-breath you draw down silver sparks of energy from the heavens. Feel the two different energies meeting at your Hrit chakra, coalescing and being transmuted, empowering you with their energy. Feel the energy building up within you as you become the axis mundi, the connection between the heavens and the earth, filled with the energy of both.

When you feel sufficiently empowered, draw your roots back from the core of the earth. Back through the rock and earth until they are completely out of the earth. Visualise yourself changing back from being a tree, and see yourself as you again. Now visualise your Hrit chakra again, and focus on the wish you want to realise and visualise all the energy you gathered at your Hrit chakra entering the wish-fulfilling tree in its centre. See the tree giving forth blossoms and a ray of white light shooting forth from the tree, out of your body and into the heavens.

CHAPTER 13

The Sri Yantra

The Sri Yantra is known as the supreme Goddess yantra (sri translates as "supreme"). Yantras are symbolic representations of deities; however the Sri Yantra represents the Goddess as all Goddesses, as the Shakti power. The Goddess is known here as Lalita, the Mother of grace, from whom all deities derive their power and authority.

It is also known as the Sri Chakra, for its intricate design is connected to the major chakras of the human body. In this way it can be seen as an interface between the human subtle energy body, and the energy of the Goddess, and it can be used as a very effective meditational tool for exploring yourself, the divine, and the relationship between you and the universe.

The Symbolism of the Sri Yantra

Although it is the supreme Goddess yantra, as it embodies the chakras, the Sri Yantra also represents the God Shiva. The four upward pointing triangles of the yantra represent Shiva, and the five downward pointing triangles represent Shakti. As there are nine major divisions formed by the nine triangles, so these correspond to nine chakras in the body. Thus two of the minor chakras are also symbolised by parts of the Sri Yantra. These minor chakras are the Lalana and Chandra upper chakras.

Muladhara chakra corresponds to the innermost downward pointing triangle, and this is also known as the *"Giver of All Accomplishments"* (Sarvasiddhiprada). In this title we can see reference to the power of Kundalini, for it is she who provides the vital force and dynamic energy in the human body, and hence is the Giver of All Accomplishments.

Svadhisthana chakra corresponds to the group of eight triangles, and is also known as the *"Remover of All Illness"* (Sarvarogahara). The sacral chakra is the centre of the emotions and of digestion, affecting many of the main organs, and hence this chakra when it is balanced and in harmony keeps the emotions and body healthy, as the Remover of All Illness.

Manipura chakra corresponds to the first set of ten triangles, and is also known as the *"Protector of All"* (Sarvaraksakara). The solar plexus chakra is the centre of will and the connection to the universe, and the will is the force which keeps boundaries clear and unwanted influences universe at bay, hence this chakra is the Protector of All.

Anahata chakra corresponds to the second set of ten triangles, and is also known as the *"Accomplisher of All Purposes"* (Sarvarthasadhaka). The heart chakra is the equilibriating point of balance and harmony in the body, and to accomplish all purposes it must be open and mediating the energy of the other chakras, thus the appropriate title.

Vishuddha chakra corresponds to the set of fourteen triangles, and is also known as the *"Provider of All Auspiciousness"* (Sarvasaubhagyadayaka). As the centre of magickal power and dreaming, this chakra provides the positive energy and insights needed for auspicious results, hence the name.

Lalana chakra corresponds to the eight petals between the inner and middle circles, and is also known as the *"Agitator of All"* (Sarvasanksakana). As the chakra which mediates the flow of spiritual energy through the body, it is self-evident why Lalana is the Agitator of All.

Chandra chakra corresponds to the sixteen petals between the middle and outer circles, and is also known as the *"Fulfiller of All Expectations"* (Sarvasaparipuraka). Chandra chakra deals with positive spiritual states which bring happiness and enable fulfilment of expectations, hence it having this title.

Ajna chakra corresponds to the outer shape, of the square with four gates that contains the rest of the yantra, and is known as the

"*Enchanter of the Triple World*" (Trailokyamohana). The Triple World is the three principles of the Gunas, representing mind, body and spirit. Ajna is the enchanter of these worlds because it is the centre of realised magickal power.

Sahasrara chakra corresponds to the central bindu (point), and is known as "*Perfect Bliss*" or "*Identical to All*" (Sarvanandamaya). As the place of the divine spark of Shiva within, the full opening of the crown chakra when pierced by the Kundalini at the end of her journey produces Perfect Bliss and dissolution of ego and identity, producing a state of removal of subject and object, where you become Identical to All.

Appendix

APPENDIX 1

Making Crystal Gem Elixirs

To make a crystal gem elixir you will need a small bowl, water (dew, distilled or mineral), the desired crystal (cleansed beforehand of course), brandy and a dark glass bottle for storage. First decide whether you wish to use sunlight or moonlight. If you are using sunlight, be sure there is a reasonable amount of sunlight, as the elixir needs a bare minimum of 3 hours sunlight. If you are using moonlight, make the elixir between the new and full moon when the moon is waxing. The crystal does not need to be large for its energies to infuse the water, so you don't need to spend large amounts on expensive chunks of crystal!

Place the crystal in the bowl of water, and place it in a window where it will catch the rays of the sun or moon. At sunset (sunlight) or sunrise (moonlight), decant the infused water into the bottle half-filling it. Top the infusion up with brandy and seal the bottle. Shake vigorously for a minute. You have now made a crystal gem elixir! Label the bottle and store it in a cool dark place. To further strengthen the elixir you may leave the crystal in the bottle with the elixir.

Whilst most crystals can be used to make crystal gem remedies, there are a few that should be avoided, because metals and minerals may leach out of the stones into the water, beyond the body's ability to process them.

The following crystals should never be used to make Gem Elizirs:
Amazonite, atacamite, auricalcite, azurite, bronchantite, chalcantite, chalcopyrite, cinnabar, conicalcite, chrysocolla, cuprite, dioptase, galena, galenite, garnierite, gem silica, lapis lazuli, marcasite, mohawkite, psiomelan, pyrite, realgar, smithsonite, stibnite, vanadanite, wulfenite.

APPENDIX 2

Glossary of Terms

Ajna	"To know", name of the sixth major chakra, located at the third eye.
Anahata	"Unstruck", name of the fourth major chakra, located at the heart.
Bhakti	"Devotion", a form of yoga.
Bindu	"Point", usually representing a manifestation of energy.
Chakra	"Wheel" or "disk", the subtle energy centres in the body.
Chandra	"Moon", also the name of a minor chakra located between the Ajna and Sahasrara chakras.
Chitrini	Nadi contained within the Vajrini Nadi, up which the Kundalini rises.
Dakini	Manifestation of Shakti in the Muladhara chakra.
Hakini	Manifestation of Shakti in the Ajna chakra.
Hatha	Type of yoga, the word is formed by combining the Sanskrit words for sun and moon.
Ida	Nadi for the lunar feminine energies.
Kakini	Manifestation of Shakti in the Anahata chakra.
Kanda	Bulb, subtle structure under the Muladhara from where all the nadis originate.
Jnana	"Knowledge", a type of yoga.
Karma	"Action", in this context a form of yoga.
Kundalini	Manifestation of Shakti as the fire serpent of creative sexual energy, residing in the Muladhara chakra.
Lakini	Manifestation of Shakti in the Manipura chakra.
Lalana	Minor chakra located at the base of the mouth.
Lingam	Sacred phallus, usually associated with the God Shiva.
Makara	A legendary animal, the fire-breathing crocodile/fish.
Maha Shakti	Supreme Shakti, manifestation of Shakti in the Sahasrara chakra.
Mala	String of 108 beads used to count recitations of a mantra.

Manas	"Mind", a minor chakra located between the Ajna and Chandra chakras.
Manipura	"Lustrous jewel", name of the third major chakra, located at the solar plexus.
Mantra	Word or sequence of words used as a means of devotion and altering consciousness.
Muladhara	"Base" or "support", name of the first major chakra, located at the perineum.
Nadi	"Flowing water" or "current", energy channels in the body.
Pingala	Nadi for the masculine, solar energy.
Pulse Point	Places on the body where the pulse can be taken, which are also good for applying essential oils, and include the wrists, temples, forehead and behind the ears.
Rakini	Manifestation of Shakti in the Svadhisthana chakra.
Sahasrara	"Thousandfold", name of the seventh major chakra, located just above the head.
Shakini	Manifestation of Shakti in the Vishuddha chakra.
Shakti	The divine feminine energy.
Shiva	The God of liberation.
Sushumna	Nadi corresponding to the spinal column, containing the six major chakras from Muladhara to Ajna.
Svadhisthana	"Sweetness", name of the second major chakra, located just under the navel.
Tantra	"Liberation", a form of yoga emphasising the polarity and union of the feminine and masculine.
Vajrini	Nadi contained within the Sushumna.
Vishuddha	"Purification", name of the fifth major chakra, located at the throat.
Yantra	A symbolic representation of a deity.
Yoni	Sacred vagina, usually associated with Shakti and represented by a downward pointing equilateral triangle.

APPENDIX 3

Safety & Allergy Cautions

Essential Oils and Herbs should always be used with caution and care should be taken to ensure their safe use. Although they are natural substances, these herbs and oils contain active chemical constituents, which though naturally occurring may interfere with other medication and have the potential to cause allergic reactions in some individuals.

For any of the following, please consult a qualified and registered practioner or your medical doctor prior to using any herbs or oils:

- o If you suffer from respiratory problems such as hayfever or asthma
- o If you suffer from heart problems, epilepsy, diabetes or any other serious health condition.
- o If you are pregnant
- o When using herbs and oils on small children or the elderly

If you are using essential oils for the first time, we recommend strongly that you first perform an allergy test. Do this by dabbing a small amount of the oil (suitably diluted) onto your skin. Leave it for 24 hours and observe for allergic reactions. If you are using an herbal tea for the first time, you may also wish to test for allergic reactions first. Do this by drinking a small amount of the tea and again wait for 24 hours and observe for allergic reactions. It is not advisable to use herbal remedies or essential oils when taking prescribed medication, unless you do so under the supervision of your medical practioner.

Please note: the advice in this book is not intended to replace the professional advice of a medical doctor or a qualified practioner. If in doubt, please always seek professional advice.

APPENDIX 4

Suppliers : Oils & Incenses

Amphora Aromatics
36 Cotham Hill
Cotham
Bristol BS6 6LA
United Kingdom
www.amphora-retail.com

Baldwin & Co
171/173 Walworth Road
London
SE17 1RW
United Kingdom
www.baldwins.co.uk

Neil's Yard Remedies
Peacemarsh
Gillingham
Dorset SP8 4EU
T: 01747 834 600
www.nealsyardremedies.com

Starchild, Glastonbury (UK)
The Court Yard
2-4 High Street
Glastonbury, Somerset
BA6 9DU
United Kingdom
www.starchild.co.uk

Bibliography

Goswami, Swami, *Layayoga – an Advanced Method of Concentration*, 1980, Routledge & Kegan Paul, London

Judith, Anodea, *Wheels of Life*, 1987, Llewellyn Publications, Minnesota

Khanna, Madhu, *Yantra: The Tantric Symbol of Cosmic Unity*, 1997, Thames & Hudson, London

Leadbeater, C.W., *The Chakras*, 1966, Ganesh and Company, Madras

Mookerjee, Ajit, *The Tantric Way: Art, Science, Ritual*, 1977, Thames & Hudson, London

Mumford, Dr John, *Ecstasy Through Tantra*, 2002, Llewellyn Publications, Minnesota

Radha, Swami Sivananda, *Kundalini Yoga for the West*, 1981, Shambhala, London

Rainbird, Ariadne & Rankine, David, *Magick Without Peers*, 1997, Capall Bann, Chievely

Shankaranarayanan, S., *Sri Chakra*, 1979, Dipti Publications, Pondicherry

Tigunait, Pandit Rajmani, *Sakti: The Power in Tantra*, 1998, Himalayan Institute Press, Pennsylvania

Vasu, Rai Bhadur Srisa Chandra, *The Siva Samhita*, 1979, Oriental Books Reprint Corporation, New Delhi

White, David Gordon, *Kiss of the Yogini*, 2003, University of Chicago Press, Chicago

Woodroffe, Sir John, *The Serpent Power*, 2003, Ganesh and Company, Madras

-----------, *Tantra of the Great Liberation*, 1978, Dover, New York

-----------, *The Garland of Letters*, 1985, Ganesh and Company, Madras

-----------, *Shakti and Shakta*, 1951, Ganesh and Company, Madras

Zimmer, Heinrich, *Myths and Symbols in Indian Art and Civilization*, 1946, Washington

Index

Other Books by these Authors

THE GUISES OF THE MORRIGAN
Irish Goddess of Sex & Battle – Her Myths, Powers & Mysteries
By David Rankine & Sorita D'Este
Avalonia, 2005

CIRCLE OF FIRE
The Symbolism & Practices of Wiccan Ritual
By David Rankine & Sorita D'Este
Avalonia, 2005

CLIMBING THE TREE OF LIFE
A Manual of Practical Magickal Qabalah
By David Rankine
Avalonia 2005

HEKA
The Practices of Ancient Egyptian Ritual & Magic
By David Rankine
Avalonia 2006

ARTEMIS – Virgin Goddess of the Sun & Moon
A comprehensive study of the Greek Goddess of the hunt, her powers, myths
and worship.
By Sorita D'Este
Avalonia, 2005

BECOMING MAGICK
New & Revised Magicks for the New Aeon
By David Rankine
Mandrake of Oxford, 2004

CRYSTALS – Healing & Folklore
The symbolism & myths of crystals
By David Rankine
Capall Bann, 2001

Other Books in this Series:

Avalonia's Book of Magick Numbers
A Practical Manual To Working With Numbers In Magick – Including Numerology, Gematria,, Dice Divination, Magick Number Squares & Much More.

Avalonia's Book of Lunar Rites
A Practical Manual For Working With The Magick Of The Moon - Includes Workings With Archangels, Gods & Goddesses, Moon Raking,, Silver Coin Spells And Many Other Lunar Magicks.

Avalonia's Book of Astral Journeys
A Practical Manual To Working In The Astral Realms - Includes Techniques For Astral Projection, Astral Doorways, Creating Thought Forms And Astral Temple Work.

Avalonia's Book of Planetary Magick
A Practical Manual For Working With The Magick Of The Planets - Includes Workings With The Deities Of The Planets, Archangels, Planetary Pyramid Meditations, Correspondences And Pathworkings.

Printed in the United Kingdom
by Lightning Source UK Ltd.
131663UK00001B/54/A